P9-CAL-453

CONVERSATIONS
of Miguel and Maria

LINDA VENTRIGLIA

HOW CHILDREN LEARN ENGLISH
AS A SECOND LANGUAGE
Implications for Classroom Teaching

▲ ADDISON-WESLEY PUBLISHING COMPANY
Reading, Massachusetts • Menlo Park, California
Don Mills, Ontario • Wokingham, England • Amsterdam • Bonn
Sydney • Singapore • Tokyo • Madrid • Bogota • Santiago • San Juan

Illustrations by Suzanne Bradbury.
Acknowledgment: p. 18, from *Jazz Chants for Children: Rhythms of American English through Chants, Songs and Poems* by Carolyn Graham. Copyright ©1979 by Oxford University Press, Inc. Reprinted by permission.

Library of Congress Cataloging in Publication Data

Ventriglia, Linda.
    Conversations of Miguel and María.

    Bibliography: p.
    1. English language—Study and teaching—Foreign students.   2. Children—Language.
3. Cognition in children.   4. Social interaction.   I. Title.
PE1128.A2V46   428.2′4′07   81-12783
ISBN 0-201-08147-4   AACR2

Copyright ©1982 by Addison-Wesley Publishing Company, Inc. Philippines copyright 1982.

All rights reserved. No part of this publication may be reproduced, stored in a retrieval system, or transmitted in any form or by any means, electronic, mechanical, photocopying, recording, or otherwise, without the prior written permission of the publisher. Printed in the United States of America.

ISBN 0-201-08147-4
FGHIJKLMNOPQ-MU-99876543210

Contents

To my aunt Sara R. Jasi
who sees magic in the written word

Introduction

Learning a second language is a complex task. It is not simply a matter of learning a system of rules for linking sounds and meaning; it is a dynamic process of learning to use this system for communication in a second culture.

Communication is a social process. Language and social behavior are related phenomena. Speech is an encompassing factor of the social world. The basic unit of human communication is the speech act, an intentional, verbally encoded social gesture directed by one person to another. This interactive process is described by Robert Louis Stevenson, who notes that "all speech is dead language until it finds a listener." Language is always an interpersonal means of communication defined by social situations. The strategies children rely on to produce language are thus motivated by social-communicative concerns.

A large and growing body of literature on language is devoted to social communication. Much of this literature is implicitly or explicitly concerned with studying classroom interactions. Little research, however, has been focused on what goes on *naturally* between students as they learn a second language through conversation with each other.

Conversations are the basic building blocks of language learning. It is generally found that children learn language actively as response participants in cooperative conversations. Through the use of social dialogue in conversations, children acquire the principles of syntax and knowledge of language meaning (semantics). The conversations of Miguel and María illustrate how second-language learning is accomplished in a social context. These conversations demonstrate the fact that children are strategic in approaching the task of second-language learning. Children do not learn to construct sentences in the second language at random but rather to meet social communicative needs.

The strategies outlined in this book address the following: how do children learn the second language; how do they search for information; how do they focus attention in conversations; what motivates them to practice the language; and what social functions the language fulfills. Answers to these questions are revealed through an understanding of the strategies children adopt to achieve the various goals of communication. The particular feature of the strategies is their ability to be generalized. The strategies can be used by second-language learners in various social situations to derive or to impart meaning.

The conversations in this book were gathered through naturalistic observations in classrooms across the United States where children were learning English as a second language. Children's conversations which occurred in play or classroom activities were recorded. The 450 conversations collected from such diverse native language groups as Japanese, Italian, Spanish, Chinese, Portuguese, and Haitian, were then examined for similarities. The strategies described in *Conversations of Miguel and María* occurred with high frequency in children learning English as a second language, regardless of their native language background. Conversations revealing the same strategies led to the definition of a set of presumably universal, natural language learning strategies. These are the means through which children learn and practice the second language. The strategies are labeled according to the function they serve in communication. Conversations chosen to illustrate children's strategies are presented in the context where the speech was initiated in order to show clearly how strategies were applied by children to learn the second language in a meaningful social context.

Children employ strategies to gain an explicit knowledge of word meanings and structures. A language learning strategy is defined by Bialystock (1978) as the means children use for exploiting available information to improve competence in the second language. Strategy is the method of controlling and manipulating information. Children's language learning strategies can be termed interpreters or mediators of meaning, the channel through which communication takes place. Language learning strategies constitute devices whereby children can communicate in a social situation. Strategies are put to use by children in the initial phases of second-language acquisition in meaningful social situations and are used by children to expand and refine their knowledge of the second language.

The extent to which children learn a second language is greatly influenced by their practice opportunities. Second-language learners gain a maximum exposure to the formal properties of the linguistic code as well as to the social meaning when these strategies are practiced in communicative settings with peers. Practice increases the learner's explicit knowledge of the code by the feedback he or she receives from second-language speakers. Strategies vary in the condition of use, depending on the opportunities provided children to actively pursue linguistic interactions in the classroom.

The developmental strategies presented in *Conversations of Miguel and María* are the foundations on which social strategies are based. All of the strategies in this book place emphasis on a social learning approach to the acquisition of a second language. Language learning for children is ultimately a process of bringing these strategies into conformance with the demands on the social situation. Language learning is viewed as drama, with children assuming roles of actors in social situations as they adopt strategies to practice language and to communicate in conversational settings. Basically, children learn the second language in two steps. First, they learn language receptively and then actively produce and practice language by employing the language learning strategies detailed and verified by the research in this book.

Bridging is the process whereby children tie words to concepts which are known in the first language. Pictures and actions for perception, and their word-labeling are used as a means to build extensive vocabularies.

Chunking is the strategy in which children imitate chunks of the second language. Chunks of language are phrases or units of more than one word that are unanalyzed and memorized as a whole rather than constructed. By repeating phrases holistically, children stretch their ability to communicate in social situations and learn language patterns.

Creating is the final stage of language learning in which children combine words and chunks of language creatively to express their ideas. Original sayings derived from previously learned chunks of language are the end result of this strategy.

Listening In and Sounding Out is a process used by second-language learners to develop receptive and expressive proficiency. Meaning is learned naturally by the listening action of the learner. After receptive understanding is gained, children begin to bridge this meaning over to the expressive use of the words that convey it.

Follow the Phrase is the strategy employed to utilize chunks of language in order to learn the syntax of the second language. Constant patterns and phrases are practiced by the learner and are eventually varied by changing words that follow the phrase.

Socializing is the process by which children learn social expressions holistically as chunks. Language is learned through social interaction and modified by the situation. Once the social formulas have been learned, they can be applied and practiced in other similar situations.

Cue Me In is the strategy whereby children use cues for linguistic problem solving. Cues can be visual or gestural involving sensory motor actions, linguistic or interpersonal. Children infer meaning and decode a verbal message by doing one or more of the following: paying attention to visual cues, such as concrete objects or pictures that represent the lexical item; interpreting the speaker's gestures; discerning meaning from context; using linguistic cues; and remaining alert to interpersonal feedback.

Peer Prompting is the process enabling children to learn the second language through modeling and feedback. The language learner is encouraged to experiment with the new language by imitating and repeating utterances by peers.

Wearing Two Hats is the strategy of switching to the language that the listener knows best. In this way, the student is able to convey cultural and social meaning to others.

Copycatting is the learning of the second language through affective, selective, individual, creative, and social imitation in role-play. Verbal and nonverbal patterns, selected behavior and actions, individual and creative elaborations and socially accepted expressions are dramatized in a natural context.

Putting It Together is the strategy which bridges cognitive, motivational, and social predispositions into various styles of second-language learning. Children choose different approaches to integrate their language learning experience. The language learning styles described in this strategy are:

> **Beading** • children learn a word at a time as meaning of individual words or semantics is stressed.
>
> **Braiding** • children internalize language on the level of language patterns or chunks.
>
> **Orchestrating** • children place emphasis on listening comprehension and accurate reproduction of sounds. \

Choosing the Way is an affective strategy which shows children's preferred modes of second-language learning participation. This strategy details each learner's affective or motivational style of second-language acquisition as follows:

> **Crystalizing** • children choose to maintain their identity with native

language culture and to initially reject the second language.

Crossing Over • children choose to identify with the second culture over their native culture. These children actively pursue the learning of the second language even to the extent of giving up speaking the native language in the school setting.

Crisscrossing • children choose to identify with both first and second cultures. These children easily adapt languages according to the situations they find themselves in.

The descriptions and analysis of children's natural language learning strategies, supported by the literature on second-language acquisition that are found in this book are meant to provide teachers with building blocks on which to base English as a second-language (ESL) instruction. Pedagogical implications of each strategy are noted at the end of every chapter. The teacher can thus create a learning situation congruent with students' natural learning methods. The relevance of instructional situations to language teaching is not to bring about new experience but to build on children's application of language in natural contexts. Szentivaniyi (1976) states that language teaching should stimulate natural language learning strategies. Teachers should build on what is taking place in the learning environment.

Conversational strategies give new direction for ESL instruction. The shift is away from language learning as mechanistic drills, and toward linguistic experience with social and cultural meaning. Natural strategies put into focus the notion that language study needs to match the scope and character of the second-language learner's intuitions about the nature of meaning. Meaningful use of language is, among other things, that which appropriately conveys social purpose. The behaviorist notion of drill has little connection with concepts such as meaning and purpose, which are part of conversations. Learning language holistically in the context of conversations is quite different from learning skills as separate, fragmented components of a linguistic system which often fail to convey an understanding of the intrinsic meaning. Conversations employ a whole complex of linguistic skills, whose sum of parts is less than the whole. Conversations capture the essence of second-language learning skills in single, unifying interaction patterns.

Children, however, can utilize conversations as a language learning tool only to the extent that teachers supply them with opportunities for linguistic interaction. Teachers can provide children with these opportunities by making language learning a dynamic process whereby children are continually developing their word power and their ability to express themselves linguistically.

Children should be encouraged to learn language as a conveyor of meanings rather than a system of syntactic, or even pragmatic, rules. Children learning to express themselves in a second language are ultimately acquiring a linguistic system to express themselves in a second culture.

Therefore, the interaction learners have with the social environment becomes a necessary part of the second-language acquisition process. The more language is shared, the better it is learned.

Teachers are the key figures in the classroom. They can provide children with the opportunity to develop social-expressive skills in the second language by stressing communicative principles in instruction derived from the natural language learning strategies of children.

I wish to express my gratitude to the Ford Foundation for sponsoring the writing of this book through a post-doctoral study grant at Harvard University.

I also wish to convey my appreciation to Dr. Courtney Cazden, Professor of Education, who guided my study at Harvard.

Linda Ventriglia
Boston, Massachusetts

Part I

Cognitive-Developmental Strategies and Second-Language Learning

The Name Game:
¿Qué es un Chongoléon?

Miguel wants to play a game. He discovers a group of manipulable animals in the corner of the classroom, and then finds some strawberry baskets which he imaginatively designates "cages." Miguel's game takes form, and he calls María and engages her in the "Name Game."

Miguel: Vamos a jugar con estos animalitos. Mira, si me los nombras a todos en inglés, ganas tú y puedes ponerlos en estas jaulas. Si no los nombras, gano yo.
(Let's play a game with these little animals. If you name them in English, you win and you can put them in these cages. If you don't name them, I win.)

María: Pues, yo sé todos los nombres en inglés.
(Well, I know all the names in English.)

Miguel: ¿Qué es esto?
(What is this?)

María: Un lion.

Miguel: ¿Y esto?

María: ¡Un monkey!

Miguel: ¿Y esto?

María: Un tiger.

Miguel: (Taking off the monkey's head and putting it on the lion's body.)
¿Y qué es esto?

María: (With a puzzled look) ¡Esto no es un animal!
(That isn't an animal!)

Miguel: ¡Sí es! ¿Cómo se llama?
(Yes, it is! What's its name?)

María: ¡Es un chongoleón!
(It's a monkey-lion!)

Miguel: Dímelo en inglés.
(Tell me in English.)

María: No sé.
(I don't know.)

Miguel: Te gané.
(I win.)

LABELING AND SECOND-LANGUAGE LEARNING
BRIDGING

¿Qué es un chongoleón? What is a monkey-lion? Why did María have to suddenly revert to Spanish to label Miguel's imaginary animal? María was able to name in English all the various animals presented to her by Miguel, but when faced with the cognitively and linguistically more complex task of combining two animal names to form a compound word for a new animal concept, she combined Spanish nouns. María's use of Spanish reveals that she is able to combine nouns and form abstract concepts in her first language, but as yet has not transferred this cognitive-linguistic strategy to English. A cognitive-linguistic strategy can be defined here as the interpreter or mediator, the channel through which communication takes place (Nelson 1973). **Bridging** is the strategy whereby children tie English words to concepts which are known in their first language. Children rely on pictures and actions to understand word meaning. Once meaning is understood, word labels in English are tied to concepts, thus "bridging" the way to ease of expression in the second language.

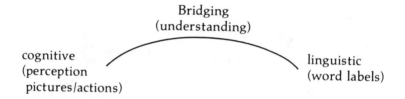

Bridging
(understanding)

cognitive
(perception
pictures/actions)

linguistic
(word labels)

Understanding/knowing (cognitive) arise in perception of the significance of labels (i.e., words) and translate to language (linguistics).

The "Name Game" Miguel was playing with María required cognitive processing of English on two levels. Firstly, the game was a simple recall task. María could play this part of the game very well. More than likely she recalled the names of the animals by rote memorization of their names in English. Secondly, the game was a problem-solving task. When Miguel constructed the imaginary animal, María was required to use language to respond by giving the more complex animal a name. Here she had to revert to Spanish, as the more complex semantic task required that María integrate two concepts (monkey and lion) and express the relationship in the form of a linguistic label. Ervin-Tripp (1974) notes that in the beginning stages of second language learning, children often fall back on first language structures to communicate at a more complex level. Thus, as María struggled to label the imaginary animal, she fell back on her first language to combine the words "chongo" (monkey) and "léon" (lion) into "chongoléon."

María's ability to abstract concepts and label them in her first language outweighs that in her second language. María's linguistic proficiency in English is currently at the point where she can express only single-word units. This is one of the beginning stages in her second-language development. Nelson (1973) explains that the child begins to learn a language by using single-word units. These express unitary and, as yet, unrelated concepts. As ability to communicate aspects of the conceptual system advances, the child will learn words and structures to express relationships among concepts.

Learning to label known objects is one of the first ways children learn a second language. Bilingual children like María come to have two names for every object. María has learned the names of the animals in Spanish, probably before coming to school; she now must rename the animals in English. The naming of objects is very important to Maria at her stage of development. Piaget (1960) has written, "Up until the age of 5 or 6, children regard a word as somehow inherent in the thing named and emanating from it." María must accomplish the strategy of Bridging by perceiving the meaning of objects, colors, shapes, sizes, states, and activities, and then labeling them in English. It has been noted by several authors that children learning a second language rely heavily on the semantic features of words. Children learn words and phrases much easier in a second language when they know their meaning. Studies by Lopez et al. (1974) indicated that bilinguals stored words in terms of the semantic representation of those words, so that the presentation of words and their translations activated the same semantic representation in memory. Meanings of words also are important because the syntactic features of sentences, such as "John hit the ball," become apparent only after the child understands the meaning of individual words (Ervin-Tripp 1974).

One problem that the bilingual child has with the meanings of words is that some words have different extensions in the two languages. For example, the English word "brush" can be used for a hairbrush, a scrubbing brush, a paintbrush, or a shaving brush. In Spanish, however, each brush has a corresponding label. A hairbrush may be labeled "un cepillo," while a paintbrush may be labeled "una brocha." In such cases, the child must learn to utilize a somewhat different set of feature markings for corresponding words in the two languages. Somehow, the child must develop a dictionary of word concepts. One of the tasks in the semantic processing of words in a second language is to attach words to their referents and then abstract concepts. The child thus must label objects and then categorize words into meaningful concepts.

The cognitive-linguistic strategy of Bridging expands the second language from perception to understanding to labeling. In Bridging, words and phrases perceptively understood through the use of imagery, symbols and interactions are expressed in language by the learner. The process of second-language acquisition without a grasp of the meaning of the utterances does not erect the bridge crossing to the other side of proficient language usage. The ease with which the meaning of the second language is derived depends upon how the strategy of Bridging is fostered in the classroom. Here we have to depend upon the skills and talents of the teacher to implement the Bridging technique by teaching words in meaningful contexts. Recurrence in meaningful situations provides the best categorization device for building a vocabulary in the second language.

IMPLICATIONS OF BRIDGING FOR SECOND-LANGUAGE LEARNING AND CLASSROOM TEACHING

The process of abstracting meaningful concepts and labeling them in the second language can be facilitated through classroom instruction that applies the Bridging strategy to the teaching of vocabulary in the following manner:

1. Present English words with concrete objects or pictures.
2. Organize vocabulary into units, grouping words by concepts.
3. Expand vocabulary words in a meaningful context.
4. Utilize all the senses in teaching vocabulary.

Presenting words with their referents, pictures, or concrete objects, permits children to tie English words to their conceptual understanding. Children know the meanings of words in their first language; they need only to give known items new labels in English. Seeing a picture or concrete object enables children to meaningfully relate these items to new English labels.

Grouping words by concepts into unit presentations develops and expands vocabulary. An example of a unit presentation is Eating Ice Cream. This unit would be taught by, first, showing children a picture of children at an ice cream store. Secondly, words relating to the picture are taught such as ice cream, cone, scooper, etc. The teacher points to each object. Thirdly, actions in the pictures are described using vocabulary words like taste, lick, and bite. Finally, vocabulary words are expanded to include flavors of ice cream, melt, sticky, etc. This unit can be made even more real by actually making ice cream as a classroom activity. Through this activity, the teacher can further expand vocabulary by teaching names of ice cream ingredients. A field trip to an ice cream store can be added as a follow-up to teach vocabulary in a real-life meaningful situation.

Involving the four senses in unit vocabulary presentations facilitates the learning of English descriptive labels. A unit on Shopping at the Grocery Store can lend itself very well to a multisensory description of vocabulary items. The teacher begins this unit by bringing fresh fruit and vegetables to class. Children are taught labels for items. Fruits and vegetables are described by color, size, and shape. Fruit and vegetables are then tasted and described as sour, sweet, etc. Touching the fruit leads to descriptions such as rough, smooth, and soft.

This descriptive unit can be expanded by showing pictures of people shopping at a store. Words such as cash register, money, and shopping cart are thus added to children's English vocabulary. Playing store with real food boxes, cans, and packages is another added experience that builds vocabulary.

Other topics that expand vocabulary in this multisensory manner are: A Trip to the Zoo; Having a Picnic; Visiting the Doctor; Going Places by Boat, Train or Car; Buying New Shoes; Building a House and Visiting a Farm.

Unit presentations can be further supplemented by vocabulary building games. The unit on foods can be followed by "Food Bingo." Children are given bingo cards with various fruit and vegetables on them. The teacher says the name of a fruit or vegetable. If children have the item on their cards they raise their hands. When the teacher calls on them each child says, "I have a pear," etc. and points to the item. If the child correctly identifies the fruit, he or she puts a marker on the bingo card. Bingos can be categorized by concept to include: animal bingo, clothing bingo and functional bingo. Functional bingo is played by putting items that are functionally related together. The teacher holds up a picture of a hammer and asks, "Who has something that goes with a hammer?" Children answer "I have a nail."

A game called "The Green Door" can also be played to encourage students to experiment with their growing vocabulary. It is played by arranging several numbered vocabulary pictures behind a large green cardboard door. The teacher describes the pictures that are hidden behind the door and gives a number to each picture. For example, the teacher might say "It has brown fur, long ears, and a white tail. Number five." Students then try to guess the name of the picture, "rabbit" and open the door to see if number five is indeed a rabbit.

Another vocabulary building game is "The Surprise Box." The teacher brings in a box of items that relate to a specific topic. For example, the teacher tells the class that the things in the box are what you use to wash with in the bathroom. One by one the items are taken out of the box and labeled: washcloth, soap, towel, and bath powder. Items are then put back in the box. The child then closes his or her eyes and reaches into the box and tries to label the thing he or she is touching.

Sequencing and categorization develops vocabulary as well. Children can be put in groups and given a large empty box from a clothing store, grocery store, etc. Children in the group are then asked to cut out items from magazines that belong in their store. The activity culminates by children in each group labeling all of the items in their store. Card games such as Concentration© and Old Maid© can also be played to develop vocabulary by matching and labeling pictures that go together.

Finally, making picture cards to illustrate the meaning of words as part of a game activity is an excellent way to personalize the learning of English vocabulary. Words like "run" can be depicted by each child in a unique way. Words that have this personalized meaning are learned faster and retained longer. Word cards from the entire class can be later grouped by concept and used to play matching games.

English vocabulary can be developed and expanded in numerous ways. The key to successful second-language learning is for the teacher to build on the Bridging strategy by presenting new words in meaningful contexts.

We Have the Technology

Miguel and María are strolling arm-in-arm to the playground, chattering happily as they walk along. They slowly make a tour of the playground and come upon a group of wooden blocks which are lying unused in a big cardboard box.

Miguel: Vamos a hacer un tren fantástico con estos bloques.
(Let's make a pretend train with these blocks.)
Pon el más grande aquí.
(Put the biggest one here.)

María: Pero necesitaremos más bloques grandes. No podremos hacerlo con los pequeños.
(But we will need more large blocks. We will not be able to make it with the small ones.)

Miguel: ¡Claro que sí! "We have the technology!"
(Yes, we can!)

USING PHRASES HOLISTICALLY
AND SECOND-LANGUAGE LEARNING
CHUNKING

Are Miguel and María two small Spanish-speaking computers? Miguel appears to have expressed in the computer-like strategy of memory retrieval the output of an English phrase (We have the technology) in an otherwise totally Spanish conversation, as if programmed to do so. But Miguel and María are not programmed computers. They are Spanish-speaking children, and Miguel has applied a sophisticated English phrase which he has not been taught directly and has applied it in a contextually appropriate manner. Miguel has remembered a "chunk" of the English language (probably heard on a television program) and has transferred it creatively and correctly to conversation.

Children learning a second language use many sophisticated structures they haven't been taught. It is not uncommon to hear phrases, such as "We have the technology," in children's verbal interactions as they begin to accumulate phrases and then apply them in conversation. This language learning strategy of "picking up" and imitating phrases in a second language may be referred to as **Chunking**.

Chunks of language are phrases or units of more than one word that are remembered as a whole. They are unanalyzed and memorized rather than constructed. The chunks of the new language serve a communicative function. Before children can speak a second language fluently, they rely on these "communicative chunks" to make themselves understood in a variety of interpersonal settings. The chunks serve as a transition from labeling in the second language to sentence fluency in that language. The phenomenon of Chunking in second-language acquisition is contrary to the usual concept of the staging of the second-language learning process. Instead of first learning grammatical rules and then generating sentences based on the rules, it was found in a study by Fillmore that the second-language learner, largely by imitation, adopts some ways of speaking first (Fillmore 1976). Children learning a second language remember and imitate verbatim chunks of language they hear in their environment.

Chunks of language convey meaning to the learner. Children use chunks of language in second language learning to do a communicative job in social situations. After imitating chunks of language, second-language learners begin to break down chunks into their component parts by coming to an understanding of the principles by which the utterances they already know how to use are structured, and only after that understanding do the learners create novel phrases of their own.

The fact is well established that children learning a second language can and do pick up chunks of language from the environment. However, the question which arises is—What causes certain chunks of language to be remembered while others are forgotten? Chunks of language which are imitated and remembered usually have meaning for the child, or can be related directly to experience. Chunks of language, as Miguel's "We have the technology," are learned in a meaningful context, such as a television program or through active social interaction, and not in isolation. Thus, for a teacher to drill students on this particular chunk of language, isolated from context, would relegate this phrase to meaningless gibberish. After such a drill, children like Miguel probably would not be heard using this language chunk because it would convey no meaning to them. Hearing the phrase, "We have the technology," while viewing a cartoon or puppet show where the meaning is relevant to the action taking place, puts the chunk into perspective for Miguel. The sequence of action in which the words are used is interesting to Miguel and therefore he remembers the new chunk of language, which he imitates and transfers to an interaction with a friend. Meaningful chunks of language therefore are duplicated by children as they are learning a new language. Language chunks are reiterated in social interactions where they make sense. "We have the technology" was heard by Miguel and later used in a situation probably having aspects similar to the one in which he heard it.

Language can be thought of as a tool for children, and the usefulness of the tool is related to how children can use language to describe concrete experiences, as well as to relate to the world. Children learning a second language receive language input from their environment and selectively imitate those phrases, or chunks of language, that have meaning for them and that they need to interact socially with others. Children use language chunks again and again, holistically, to convey or obtain information until they become more familiar with the language. Chunking is used by second-language learners as the second step after labeling, before transition to the further step of creating novel utterances of their own by breaking down chunks and figuring out principles of how the language is constructed.

IMPLICATIONS OF CHUNKING FOR SECOND-LANGUAGE LEARNING AND CLASSROOM TEACHING

Two main approaches are used in language curricula for second-language learning—Habit Formation and Creative Construction. Habit Formation is an approach to learning taken from behaviorist psychology (Skinner 1957). This method sets forth the belief that just as rats can be conditioned to pick up a disk or pigeons to push a button, children can be taught chunks of language through a similar stimulus-response model. In accordance with this method, a lesson begins by giving children a stimulus, such as a picture of a banana, and the stimulus language chunk—"What is this?" The teacher then models the response chunk—"This is a banana." The children repeat, "This is a banana." The chunk, "This is a," is then used as the response to various fruit. Each time the children are presented with the stimulus of a picture of a fruit and the stimulus chunk words "What is this?" they respond "This is a (banana, pineapple, etc.)." Later, the children are presented with "an" apple and they respond with the conditioned response chunk, "This is a apple." The teacher quickly corrects the children, saying "This is an apple." The children thereby are given a new chunk of language which must be conditioned until it becomes a habit. It is hoped that chunks of language learned in this drill will be transferred to other language situations.

Much to the detriment of the teacher's efforts, however, the transfer of drill phrases to social interactions often is nil and fails. Students not only do not use structures they have just practiced successfully in drills, there also appears to be no transfer to natural communicative settings. These facts were explicitly demonstrated in one classroom at lunchtime. The teacher had just finished the drill pattern, "This is a (an)" with the appropriate names of various types of fruit, and most conveniently, apples were served for lunch. The teacher expectantly picked up an apple and asked one child, "What is this?" The child not only did not respond with the chunk, "This is an apple," but replied hesitantly, "Quiero la más grande." The answer the child gave was a meaningful response but, unlike the learned drill phrase, communicated a desire appropriate to the situation. The child wanted the bigger apple.

This kind of situation manifests what is most conspicuously absent from drill/habit formation lessons. These drills are intended to teach the forms of the English language and not to convey information about the real world. The meaning or concept is therefore secondary to the repetition of the stated form. McLaughlin (1978) states that learning depends not so much on repetition as it does on the students' awareness of the meaning of what is drilled. The chunks of language taught in a drill do give children a model of correct syntax, but often carry no message at all, much less a message that can be transferred to the world which lies outside the twenty-minute language lesson. Content in most language drills is subverted to mechanics, and thus the thoughts conveyed do not incite the interest of the children and fail to transfer to everyday language usage.

In the Creative Construction approach, children use chunks of language in the context of an activity (Burt and Dulay 1975). Interactions with peers and with the teacher allow children to hear and repeat chunks of language that are relevant to the task that is being carried out. The teacher models language chunks as she or he interacts with small groups of children. Language chunks are learned as they relate to the content of the activity. Children imitate language chunks throughout the activity.

The Creative Construction model was manifested in one classroom where children in small groups of five to six were tracing each other's feet and then cutting out the tracings. The children were asked to find the biggest foot in the group, and later to sequence the feet from the biggest to the smallest. The teacher showed concrete examples of feet and modeled the language chunks: "This foot is big." "This foot is bigger." "This foot is biggest." Children could be heard using the language chunk, "This foot is bigger," to describe each other's feet. The teacher passed the groups and looked at the children's feet cut-outs, picked them up, and sequenced them, commenting "This foot is big; This foot is bigger; This foot is biggest," thus reinforcing the language chunks modeled previously, and having the children repeat them. Children were laughing and joking about big feet, but also learning the language forms big, bigger, and biggest in the context of a concrete math activity. Later, at lunchtime, these same children were seen arguing about who had been given the biggest cookie, repeating the same language chunk, "This is biggest," that they had used earlier in the planned activity and transferring it to another social setting.

The implementation of the Creative Construction method for second-language learning implies four strategies for classroom instruction. First, the teacher must be a creative observer of the natural communication which transpires in child-directed activity. The teacher must listen carefully to how children use language and note under what conditions. Secondly, the teacher must be a creative designer of content activities which closely approximate natural social interactions. Language in the creatively designed tasks accompanies natural hands-on activities, such as science experiments, games, arts and crafts. Thirdly, the teacher must allow each child the opportunity to imitate the language chunks he or she hears in meaningful activities of small groups, using concrete materials wherever possible, in order that the child can ultimately become a creative constructor with both materials and language. Arranging children in small groups allows each child the opportunity to practice repeating given language chunks that accompany activities. Listening, practicing, and repeating are the means by which children learn their first language, and these processes should be employed in second-language learning as well (Palmer 1968). Children in small groups also learn language chunks from each other in the course of group interaction. Finally, the teacher acts as a creative model, constructing appropriate language chunks and responding to each child's repetition of chunks by reinforcing and validating verbal responses. Language chunks learned in this way do transfer to other situations because they are connected to personal and interpersonal experience. Language is, after all, a complex set of meaningful relations which function as a structure for human interaction. Most generally, the goal of second-language instruction in the early grades is to give children a facility with, and experience in, the language that will raise the level of communication (McLaughlin 1978).

Language chunks transmit meaning first as an accompaniment to concrete, physical activity, and later this is transferred to similar experiences. Ultimately, language chunks are integrated into sentence patterns which the child creates and recreates as he or she develops communicative fluency. The Creative Construction method facilitates the transfer of language chunks by giving the child opportunities to imitate and use language in meaningful social contexts. The success of the learner's efforts will depend upon the input he or she gets, and the variety of contexts in which he or she is exposed to the new language.

Can the Habit Formation method encourage language transfer? Drills which are not sterile and totally removed from personal relevance may, in fact, have transfer value. Drills which are used in game-like situations where children are actively using language may be very beneficial. Language chunks tied to a game situation take on meaning.

Games such as "Going Places" can be played to learn language chunks. In this game, children illustrate places they would like to go (the store, movies, park, etc.). The teacher models a question: "Where do you like to go?" The instructor also models the chunk to describe individual students' pictures, "to the park, to the store, and to the movies." The teacher repeats the question and through choral response children repeat the chunk, "to the" with individually selected vocabulary words. The class is then divided into two teams. The teacher poses the question. Team members answer in relation to the pictures that are used (to the park, to the store, etc.) and score a point for their teams.

Social greetings are among the first chunks of language mastered by second-language learners. These chunks are readily learned because of their transfer value to many social situations. Thus, a game called "Greetings," consisting of a game board with pictures of different people in various social settings, is of great use in the classroom. Children must give the social greeting chunk of language that describes the action. "Good morning," would describe the picture of a man in his pajamas greeting the paperboy or girl. "How are you?" is the greeting that matches the picture of a person visiting a patient in the hospital. The teacher explains each picture and then instructs children by having them repeat modeled social greeting chunks that match the pictures. Later, greetings are used in the form of a game where children roll a die and move their marker to a picture on the game board. The child must give the social greeting that matches the picture he or she has landed on. If the child correctly states the greeting, the marker is left on the picture; if not, the marker cannot be moved.

Chants also can be used in a game-like situation to encourage the learning of chunks in the second language. Graham (1979) in her book *Jazz Chants for Children* includes a number of these chants. The chunks of language "Good morning" and "I don't know" are learned in a chant about Ernie. The chant is:

Good morning.
  Hello.

Good morning.
  Hello.

Where's Ernie?
  I don't know.

Where's Ernie?
  I don't know.

Good morning.
  Hello.

Good morning.
  Hello.

Where's Ernie?
  I don't know . . .

The rhythm and flow of chants such as this one enables children to learn chunks of the English language in a stimulating game-like situation. Chunks learned in this way are meaningfully transferred to social settings. The chunk "Good morning" is utilized as a greeting for social encounters. The chunk "I don't know" can be used as a response to questions when the answer is not known.

The end goal of learning a second language is to speak it appropriately and creatively in varied social contexts. This goal can be encouraged and facilitated in a classroom that uses language as the key to open the door of communication within the human family.

New Red Boots
and Old Blue Tennis Shoes

The teacher has been using picture cards for a number of weeks for "The English Game." She uses variations of this game to teach English labels and chunks of language to Spanish speakers in her class. She has grouped the picture cards in the categories of people, animals, transportation vehicles, clothing, food, toys, and colors. She has taught vocabulary words relating to each category with a preceding language chunk that is repeated throughout the game with each new vocabulary word. Thus, when the children were learning clothing names they repeated, "I wear," "I wear shoes," "I wear boots," etc. Food items were preceded by "I eat" and toys by "I play with."

The teacher in this dialogue is teaching attributes to accompany the vocabulary children already know, such as big, pretty, old, and new. The teacher has selected the attributes of old and new to start the instruction. She uses pictures of pairs of objects that are old or new with the language chunk, "These are," to introduce the attributes.

The teacher has created a game situation by using a game board. The game board has two doors that open. One door is obviously old, the other is new. Behind the doors are small pictures that match the picture cards the teacher is using in the exercise. After the child has labeled the object old or new, he or she looks behind the chosen old or new door to check his or her response by matching the large picture to the small picture behind the door. If the response is correct, the card is held up and the child keeps the card. At the end of the game, the children count their cards. The child with the most cards wins the game.

After the lesson, the teacher expanded the concept taught in the lesson by having informal conversations with children as the means to the end of having children engage in creative language production.

Teacher: Vamos a jugar un juego en inglés. Aquí yo tengo unas cosas. Algunas son nuevas, otras son viejas. Díganme si son nuevas o viejas. Voy a decir:—"¿Qué son estos?" Me van a decir: "Estos son viejos o estos son nuevos."

Let's play a game in English. Here I have some things. Some are new, others are old. I will say—"What are these?" You tell me—"These are old, or these are new."

(Directions are explained in Spanish and in English.)

Teacher: What are these?
(Showing two old shoes)

María: These are old.

Teacher: What are these?
(Showing two new houses)

Miguel: These are new.

The group disperses but Miguel and María remain. The teacher engages the children in conversation.

Teacher: I'm going to buy some new shoes. These are old.

María: (Looks down at her feet and says to the teacher)
          These are new red boots.

Miguel: (laughing—looks down at his feet and says)
          These are old blue tennis shoes.

CREATIVE CONSTRUCTION
AND SECOND-LANGUAGE LEARNING
CREATING

How are new red boots like old blue tennis shoes? What do Miguel and María's sentences have in common? The sentences Miguel and María created after the language lesson were unlike any of the sentences they had heard or spoken in the game; the sentences are creative language constructions. They used words they had learned previously, combined them with the chunks of language introduced by the teacher (These are old. These are new.), to create two novel utterances that are inherently meaningful. This process of formulating original utterances from previously learned words and chunks of language is referred to as **Creating** with language.

Creating is an integrative process of language learning by which children build new sentence structures based on grammatical patterns that they come to internalize. The perceptual understanding of words and the conceptual understanding of chunks of language form the base that results in the creation of a novel sentence structure.

Miguel and María began learning the second language of English without any understanding of its underlying structure. They learned phrases or chunks of language as well as individual words, and used them holistically in social interactions without knowledge of the internal structure of the speech segments. As Miguel and María began to acquire a repertory of such expressions, they began to look for recurring parts in the formulas, or chunks of language they knew. This was the beginning of their syntactic development in English. Their adventure into the language began leading them to discover that constituents of the chunks of language they had learned were inter-changeable and combinable; therefore, "These are new," "These are boots," and "These are red" could become "These are new red boots." By determining the parts of the chunks of language that could be varied, the children could begin Creating with language. The children, after freeing elements from the original chunk, had an abstract structure consisting of a pattern or rule by which the creation of their novel utterances became possible.

Fillmore (1976) studied five young Spanish speakers learning English as a second language and found that they began to learn the language by memoriz-ing chunks of language as unanalyzed wholes. Later, these chunks were broken down by the children to construct many new sentences. The chunk of language, "How do you do this?" eventually began to be used by the children in constructed sentences such as, "How do you do this puzzle?" or "How do you do this dance?", and then, "How do you make these little tortillas?" or "How do you make a flower?" Finally, "how" was freed and the children constructed the sentences: "How do you make it?" and "How will you take off the paste?"

Thus, "how" came to be analyzed progressively until only the question word remained. The children then were able to construct a large variety of questions that could be used in a variety of situations. The children in Fillmore's study came to know more and more about the English language by using its structures, first holistically, and then by breaking down the structures and analyzing them into their component parts.

Miguel and María also are beginning to come to know the English language, and the strategy of Chunking that served them well initially for communication purposes is now becoming a background for Creating. The process of Creating is a necessary progressive step to communicating in the language. How could Miguel and María communicate effectively if they had to depend on a set of sentences stored in their minds from which they would choose when they wanted to say something? Even if they had stored an enormous number of these sentences in what is termed the computer-brain, the possibility of immediate recall of the apt sentence would be very difficult, if not impossible. In order to communicate adequately, sentences must be created to fit the social interaction. Each spoken sentence must be created anew to express and communicate to particular individuals, oneself, or others (Cazden 1972). Because language is so situation-specific, few sentences are spoken or heard more than once; that is, each language utterance is unique and meaningful to the context in which it is verbalized. Chomsky (1966) states, "The heart of human language capability is creativity in expressing and understanding meanings, free from control of external stimuli and appropriate to new and ever-changing situations."

This Creating process in second-language acquisition has been defined further by Burt and Dulay (1975) as "a process in which children gradually reconstruct rules for the speech they hear, guided by universal innate mechanisms which cause them to use certain strategies to organize that linguistic input, until the mismatch between the language system they are exposed to and what they produce is resolved." The second-language learner's construction of linguistic rules can be regarded as creative because no native speaker of the second language, whether peer, parent or teacher, models many of the kinds of sentences produced regularly by children who still are learning the basic syntactic structures of a language.

Hakuta (1975) comments on this creative process of second-language learning by describing a Japanese child's acquisition of English. The child first attended selectively to all the talk around her, enlarging her repertoire of utterances understood. She then tested her conception of words and sentences by trying out chunks of language on her peers and on other adults in the environment, and awaited their acceptance or rejection. Hakuta reported that later the girl began to break down chunks of language she had learned holistically and to use language creatively. The girl progressed from utterances such as, "I don't know where is the money," to "I don't know where it is," to "I don't know where the bathroom is."

Hatch (1978) described another Japanese child's acquisition of English as a second language. She noted that at first the child took particular interest in learning chunks of language. Subsequently, these expressions were broken down and used creatively. "I wanna" first appeared in utterances as "I wanna orange juice" and "I wanna drive." Later, forms such as, "I wanna down" and "I wanna cake" appeared. Ultimately, the child said, "I want to play" and "I want to open it." Thus, the child progressed in acquiring English much like the other children described, from using language imitatively to creatively constructing utterances.

Piaget's (1960) notions of assimilation and accommodation may be relevant to the processes described in the creating process by which a child interprets some of the speech forms around him or her and then eventually works them into his or her own grammatical system. Creating with second language indeed can be thought of as an integrative process at work. The child learning a second language comes to know the language, much as he or she comes to see the total visual image after putting a puzzle together. As the child begins to put together the puzzle, he or she starts out with chunks of the puzzle which are different sizes and shapes, just as the beginning second-language learner starts out with memorized chunks of language of different lengths and meanings. The child then begins to put together the puzzle chunks, just as the second-language learner begins to creatively put together language forms. Finally, the child fits all the pieces together and sees the whole picture, just as the child learning a second language puts together grammatical forms to create a whole linguistic system.

IMPLICATIONS OF <u>CREATING</u> FOR SECOND-LANGUAGE LEARNING AND CLASSROOM TEACHING

Miguel and María demonstrated, when they created the sentences, "These are new red boots," and "These are old blue tennis shoes," that they had attained meaning from the language. The teacher in the preceding example, by teaching chunks of language in a meaningful game situation followed by individual conversations, allowed the children to gain an understanding of the English words, old and new, as well as the grammatical structure (chunk). This understanding led the children to tie the chunk to other words and ultimately create novel utterances.

Children acquiring a second language, as Miguel and María, appear to learn language best in conversations or in game-like situations where language is used meaningfully and is associated with some concrete reference at the beginning, such as objects or pictures. They can become full participants in conversations from the beginning, when the teacher responds to their intended meaning. The teacher pays attention, then, to what the children are trying to say, not to how they are saying it. The teacher also helps the second-language learners by expanding their statements and modeling correct language forms. Various conversational activities, such as role-playing situations, are devised by the teacher to engage children in hearing and using the language. As the child learns to speak the second language, first by imitating chunks of language and then by breaking down the chunks to form creative utterances, their successive attempts at interacting with language should be evaluated, not according to their conformity to the rules of full native language competence, but according to their consistency with the children's interim grammars. Interim grammars should be considered as trial hypotheses children use when trying to discover the grammatical patterns of a second language. Children should be given opportunities to perceive and practice these patterns in meaningful ways. This connotes the fact that every language learning activity is immediately a meaningful communication experience. A truly communicative environment is one in which children are most likely to learn the regularities, patterns or rules that make possible development from imitating chunks of language to creating language structures.

Second-language learners internalize language rules on the basis of patterns acquired in social interactions (Gough 1967). Hatch (1978) states that the acquisition of a second language (like a first language) evolves out of learning how to carry on a conversation. To communicate with others, children must learn how to identify the topic of conversation and how to keep it going. Asking for clarification, repetition, imitation, eliciting vocabulary, and guessing are strategies second-language learners use to carry on a conversation. It is well for teachers to understand that through such conversational strategies children learn to interact with others verbally and eventually develop syntactic structures of the language.

If it is acknowledged that meaningful conversational practices are so important in learning a second language, then classroom curriculum must be created which allows children to engage in as many language interactions as possible. Language activities must concentrate on highly specific interactions in the uses of language, rather than on situationally empty pattern drills. Language in the classroom should be thought of primarily as a medium of communication and therefore must be learned in the context of a communicative act.

The question which now arises is—What kinds of classroom activities encourage this type of language learning? Channeled conversations are one of the best mediums for children to develop the creative use of the second language. This technique allows the teacher to structure small group activities around various meaningful conversational topics. For example, the topic Building a Village actualizes creative language usage as children talk about what they are doing while building an Eskimo village out of sugar cubes or an

Indian village out of mud. The teacher builds on creative language by commenting on group activities and engaging children in communication about what they are doing.

The game Clue© reinforces channeled conversations as the child verbally decides where the crime happened, who committed the crime, and why the character did it.

Story telling through picture strips is another way to encourage creative conversations. Children can arrange picture strips to tell a story and later relate the story to the class.

Imaginary situations in the game "What If?" stimulate creative language. Questions posed to students include:

What if everything in the world were green?

What if alligators had birds for babies?

What if Christmas was every day?

Children can answer these questions in small groups. They also can illustrate their answers by drawing a large group mural.

All these game activities encourage the development of the creative use of the second language. Learning environments in the classroom should be created to reactivate the natural language learning abilities children have. The following criteria should be considered for structuring second-language instruction where conversation is the means to the end of creative language production.

1. The learner is allowed to progress from imitating chunks of language to forming a set of increasingly complete rules about the second language.

2. Perception of patterns is emphasized rather than intensity of practice.

3. The learner is encouraged to produce sentences that are ungrammatical in terms of full native competence so that feedback might be obtained about the adequacy of inductively formulated rules (Cook 1969).

4. The teacher responds to content of what the child says rather than to grammatical structures.

5. Teaching techniques involve using language patterns in game-like situations, partial repetition of sentences, verbal play, and situationally appropriate expansions of the learner's sentences.

6. Language lessons are structured around interpersonal communication in meaningful situations.

Perhaps of most importance when considering second-language acquisition as a Creative Construction process is the realization that language is integrated in all subject-matter teaching. Language is used to teach math, reading, science, art, etc. Language is not an isolated subject to be taught only during a twenty-minute segment of the day. Children learn the structures and meanings of the linguistic forms of the second language in meaningful contexts across subject-matter disciplines. They learn to communicate in the second language all day long through verbal interactions with peers and with adults. The teacher who encourages the creating process in the classroom listens, watches, models, and expands language throughout the day. Second-language learners can establish their own categories and grammatical rules for the language by being encouraged to experiment with language. To the extent that children are persuaded to use language will they become creators with the potential to make an original contribution to our understanding of the world.

Part II

Social-Affective Strategies and Second-Language Learning

Jump In and Say

Every day for a week María could be seen at recess watching the other children play jump rope. She didn't participate, but stood close enough to observe and to "listen in" to the jump rope rhyme that the children were chanting.

On the first day of the second week, María took her usual stance a few feet away from the game, but now she wasn't just standing passively watching the game, she could be seen "sounding out" to herself the words of the jump rope rhyme.

> *"Juu-mp, Juuu-mp in and saay*
> *One-un-un, two-ooo, threee,*
> *Juu-mmp in wi-th me."*

María repeated the words over and over taking delight in saying them louder, softer, and with different stress. After playing with the individual sounds of the words, María repeated the rhyme several times putting the sounds of the words together.

María paused after the first repetition and listened again to the other children. She appeared to be checking her vocalization against theirs. Then she smiled, said the rhyme again, matching the words to the actions of the children. Finally, she sought out a jump rope and went to look for Miguel.

María: (jumping rope):
Jump in and say
One, two, three,
Jump in with me.

Miguel: ¿Qué dices?
(What are you saying?)

María: Quiero que tú brinques conmigo.
(I want you to jump with me.)

Brinca y di
Uno, dos y tres,
Brinca conmigo.

Jump in and say
One, two, three,
Jump in with me.

Miguel: One, two, three . . .
María: Jump in with me.
Miguel: Jump in with me.
María: Jump in and say
One, two, three,
Jump in with me.

RECEPTIVE EXPRESSIVE STRATEGY
AND SECOND-LANGUAGE LEARNING
LISTENING IN AND SOUNDING OUT

"Jump in and say, but not right away." This rhyme seems to appropriately describe the natural language learning strategy María applies to develop her receptive and expressive proficiency in English. This strategy can be labeled **Listening In and Sounding Out.**

Initially, María appears to be learning the language receptively by listening intently to the jump rope rhyme, tying the children's actions to the words, and so understanding the meaning of the words. She observes one, two, three jumps and hears the accompanying words. After María has gained a receptive understanding of the words, she begins to use her expressive language ability to play with the sounds of the individual words. She isolates individual sounds and later combines them into larger word units to gain a "feel" for the words. Playing with the sounds of the words is not María's ultimate goal. Her goal is to derive meaning from the words. Therefore, she says the words in time to the actions of the other children. Her mastery of the meaning of the words is apparent from the fact that she is able to translate the words for Miguel to teach him the jump rope rhyme.

The strategy of Listening In and Sounding Out, therefore, can be viewed as the process María exercises to ultimately derive meaning from the words of the jump rope rhyme. Once María has attained a receptive understanding of the words, she can bridge this meaning over to the special words that convey it. Because she is able to express the words with meaning, they become part of her verbal repertoire and can be transferred to another social context with Miguel.

Listening In and Sounding Out, as a process, brings together the two critical skills necessary to master a second language: listening comprehension and expressive fluency. María's approach of "listening in" before "sounding out" lends support to the theory that receptive language precedes expressive language development in the achievement of communicative competence. There is considerable evidence, both anecdotal and experimental, in first and second language acquisition studies, indicating that language competence, including productive competence, is learned first through receptive means— that is, through listening. For example, in first-language acquisition, Lenneberg (1967) cites evidence that normal children learning their first language demonstrate comprehension of sentences at least six months before demonstrating readiness to speak.

Research studies on second-language acquisition also have manifested that children often prefer to concentrate on their receptive skills for an extended period of time before producing language. Ervin-Tripp (1974) concludes that the process of second-language acquisition looks much like first-language acquisition in natural situations. She describes thirty-one English-speaking children, ages 4-9, in a Swiss school where the language of instruction was French. She notes that children listened for sometimes as long as several months before they started speaking. The results of this study serve to further strengthen the theory that children develop receptive language skills before skills of oral expression.

Sorenson, an anthropologist, studied Colombian and Brazilian Indian children learning a second language. He states, "The Indians appear to utilize the most effective strategy they know for learning language—delaying oral production until reaching an appropriate state of readiness." (Sorenson 1967). He concludes that listening before speaking might be termed a natural second-language acquisition strategy.

Sorenson's results may be explained by pointing out that initially the child learning a second language must concentrate on processing the language around him receptively to gain an understanding of the words. The child becomes so engrossed in this process that he can concentrate on only one dimension of language at first, which is the receptive one. This statement is supported by María's behavior. She watches the jump rope game for a week, so engrossed in listening to the words to gain an understanding that she not only doesn't speak at first, she doesn't even participate in the game.

A number of experimental studies have shown that it is possible to accelerate the rate of acquiring listening comprehension when second-language listening training precedes oral practice. Emphasis on such listening training has been shown to contribute to the development of oral fluency. Postovsky (1970) in two twelve-week studies, compared a delayed oral response approach with an audiolingual approach to second-language learning, where students were required to mimic what they had heard from the first day on. The experimental group who were given only a receptive exposure to the language proved superior in listening comprehension, and ultimately in productive skills. Thus, it may be concluded from these results that concentration on receptive language learning initially facilitates the development of expressive language skills.

Asher's studies also have revealed the benefit of listening training. Asher (1966) advocates what he terms the Total Physical Response technique for teaching language through listening. This technique utilizes a method in which students are not required to respond verbally. Students listen, for example, to a command in the second language and then immediately respond, along with the instructor, with an appropriate physical action. Students are required to tune in or "listen in" carefully to the commands in order to make an appropriate physical response. Asher's (1972) work has demonstrated that second-language learning can be accelerated through the development of listening comprehension. Asher has noted that there seems to be a relatively high degree of positive transfer from listening skills to expressive language skills. Carroll (1973) also has confirmed Asher's finding by noting that listening comprehension training improves student mastery of a second language.

These studies serve to illustrate that the natural strategy María employed of listening in before speaking is in actuality the preferential approach of most second-language learners. While this fact has been confirmed by many research studies, most modern ESL methodologies in practice require that the productive skill of speaking be mastered along with the receptive skill of listening. Thus, while students may be asked to produce only what they already have heard, they will be required to do so almost immediately after having heard it (Gary 1975).

This approach is contrary to the research findings and to the natural language acquisition strategy used by María of "listening in" before "sounding out." Immediate oral practice of meaningless phrases often is imposed on children learning a second language. This instantaneous oral practice often does not expedite the development of productive and receptive oral competence in the second language because the children many times bring to this practice no perceptual understanding of the words. They are practicing, like parrots, words they do not understand. Indeed, for many learners, delaying oral practice may be preferable, both from an affective viewpoint and from the point of view of language acquisition theory.

In order to effectively speak a language, children must feel ready. They must be given time to experience the language in natural social contexts. They must accustom themselves to a new code of response. María accustomed herself to the new English code by spending time listening. It was only after María gained a perceptual understanding of the words that she was able to comprehend, internalize, and later repeat these same words in another appropriate context.

Second-language learners must perceive some comprehension of the language system they are trying to internalize. Meaning must be linked to the spoken words. Cazden (1972) states that "meaning is the most important of all aspects of language." If induced to speak before they have gained a perceptive understanding of the language, children will be distracted from their main goal—learning the underlying system, as deemed a prerequisite for the use of language. A receptive understanding of language allows children to bridge meaning to the words they hear in social contexts. Expressive fluency follows, as children then verbalize the words that communicate the meaning.

From the foregoing discussion, it may be stated that receptive understanding leads to expressive production naturally. The strategy used by María of Listening In and Sounding Out reveals how this transition takes place as part of a language learning process. In order to more fully understand language learning as a process, the "listening in" part of the strategy cannot be looked at in isolation but only as it relates to the second part of the process, "sounding out."

María begins the expressive part of the process by "sounding out" word parts. She engages in "sound play," much as a child does when learning a first language by elongating the sounds of consonants and vowels, and later changing rhythm, volume, and intonation. Garvey (1974) talks about sound play as being one of the first ways a child learning his or her native language expresses himself or herself. Sound play includes volume escalation, changes in speed, and drawing out significant utterances.

Recordings of solitary children learning a first language show long episodes of vocal modulation of words. Repetitive, rhythmic vocalizations are used in early language play. Children appear to link vocalizations to motor activities. Chanting and rhyming can be heard in a sing-song rhythm. In all these types of playful vocalizations, the meaning is secondary to the sound at first. Weir (1962) taped the monologues of her son learning a first language and found many examples of sequences of utterances where play with language sounds seemed primary. Children may then be said to use a "sounding out" strategy to engage in verbal play. This ultimately leads to the development of expressive language. Bruner (1972) notes that many skills are first developed and practiced in play.

María's strategy of sounding out the words of the jump rope rhyme initially is not unlike the process first-language learners use in developing communicative competence. At first, María seems to be enjoying playing with the sounds of the words that comprise the jump rope rhyme. However, as she plays with the sounds, it can also be noted that she is tuned in to the actions of the children. She begins to shift her emphasis from paying attention to the sounds alone to tying them to the meaning they express. Attention to sounds, thus, in the beginning stages of second-language acquisition seems to quickly shift to tying the sounds to the word meaning. This fact is confirmed by the Afrikaans-English study and the Hebrew-English study. These studies found evidence that bilinguals are capable at an earlier age of separating the meaning of a word from its sound (Ben-Zeev 1977).

Another study by Nedler (1975) pointed to the necessity of learning sounds of the new language as they are related to word meaning. In his study, a phonetic approach was used to teach Spanish-speaking children English. Words were isolated in English and Spanish that had similar sounds, and then taught to the children in a rote manner. The goal was to produce accent-free speech. The result was dubious mastery of fragmented vocabulary which was of little use for communication or thought. Nedler concluded that central to learning the sounds of a language for the bilingual is the meaningfulness of the sounds. Thus, teaching sounds alone in a meaningless manner does not expedite the expressive abilities of bilinguals, and often delays oral production. Sounds are learned for effective usage in communication only as part of a process that ties sounds to words and phrases receptively understood. As Ervin-Tripp (1977) notes, sounds are important to formulate words, but knowledge of meaning is basic to communication.

María's use of sounding out in the repetitious sequence of the rhyme gave her much redundant information that eventually allowed her to make associations from word sounds to word meanings. María practiced the words with two goals in mind—firstly to relate them to her receptive understanding, and then secondly, to be able to express them so she could join in the jump rope play interactions. Ervin-Tripp (1977) states that for a child the meaning of a word is related to the act of social interpretation. María's strategy of Listening In and Sounding Out then can be seen as a total process in her effort to gain receptive meaning from the second language in order that she might express the words effectively in social interactions.

IMPLICATIONS OF <u>LISTENING IN AND SOUNDING OUT</u> FOR SECOND-LANGUAGE LEARNING AND CLASSROOM TEACHING

Instructional strategies that teach children a second language should proceed from receptive understanding to expressive practice. Asher's (1966) Total Physical Response technique can be used in a variety of imaginative ways to give students practice in appropriately responding to what they hear. For example, in a game of "Simon Says," students can demonstrate comprehension of commands by such gross motor acts as walking, pointing, jumping, moving parts of the body or picking up things. Asher's technique is one way of teaching a great deal of beginning language through the receptive mode. Delayed oral practice to initial second-language learning combined with a physical response mode can be effective both for developing listening skills and for developing oral competence, given an extended period of active listening practice.

Listening activities can thus be viewed as an integral or core part of the second-language curriculum. Group activities could include the telling of stories or the showing of films sequenced according to content. These activities would be followed by comprehension questions sequenced according to grammatical and semantic structure and designed to elicit nonverbal responses.

Individual activities could include listening to records or tapes accompanied by visual aids. A listening post with headsets is an excellent way for children to tune into language by hearing a story that accompanies a picture book they have before them. Command tapes also build on receptive language. Children first are taught by the teacher the command used on the tape, such as, "Put a circle around . . ." Children are then given a worksheet with pictures in rows. The tape begins by having the child point to each picture as the label is given in English. Then the children listen and respond to the command, "Put a line under the chair." heard on the tape. Other similar commands are: "Draw a square around the monkey." "Color the house red." etc.

Using pictures and objects to teach language comprehension is also appropriate because it provides learners with visual, as well as auditory, input. Receptive activities conducted in small groups could consist of commands such as, "María, pick up the picture of the dog and put it next to the lady." Pencil and paper activities can prove to be an effective strategy in which to reinforce directions as well. The teacher can instruct the students to draw certain figures and then have them elaborate upon their own illustrations. For example, "Draw a small child and a large dog. Draw a hat on the child. Next, draw a bow around the dog's neck, etc." The children can learn to listen to the directions and master the skill of listening to a series of instructions and accurately responding to the directives. The picture will become the child's final product, illustrating the many different directions in a physical format.

Much of the communication the child receives in school is in the form of directives; therefore, it is imperative that children learning a second language come to understand commands. Directives may be more easily understood by children when they unfold in the course of a physical activity rather than as unrelated commands. For example, art activities can be explained step-by-step. "Fold the paper" is thus accompanied by the children's actions of folding the paper. The teacher can go into great detail by giving the students specific commands in an activity such as this one. The teacher can actually make each direction-related activity into an adventure for the student in which they learn to listen and react to each instruction.

The expressive arts (impromptu drama, music, song, and rhymes) allow for the development of listening comprehension. Much of the literature on language acquisition has shown that children have a natural predilection for rhythm and rhyme. Rhymes are repetitious, and meaningful recurrences provide the basic categorization devices children need for learning second-language word patterns. Many rhymes and songs may be accompanied by physical activities. The strategy that the teacher would use here is to have the students listen in to the rhyme and perform the activities at first, and later say the words to accompany their actions.

Rhymes that accompany finger plays are especially liked by children. For example,

I have ten little fingers.
They all belong to me. (children hold up ten fingers).
They can do things.
Would you like to see?
I can shut them up tight. (make fist)
Open them wide. (open hands)
Put them together. (as in praying)
Make them hide. (behind back)
I can make them go high.
And make them go low, etc.

The Kimbo records distributed by Kimbo Educational in New Jersey have many rhyming songs that can be used for Listening In and Sounding Out. One of the songs is entitled, "Do You Like Foods?" The repetitiveness of the song teaches children phrases and patterns of language receptively as well as expressively, as they later say the words with the song—

"Do you like bananas? Yes, I do! Do you like bananas? Yes, I do! I like to eat my bananas. I like to eat my bananas. Do you like bananas? Yes, I do! Yes, I do!"

The song teaches the names of foods in the rhyming pattern. The teacher should show the children real or plastic fruit while they hear the words. Repetition of sound and word patterns aid the children's understanding. These songs use words in a meaningful way that holds the interest of children.

These games, songs, and activities reveal that the natural strategy of Listening In and Sounding Out can indeed be complemented in a classroom where listening comprehension is paid attention to in activities that encourage children to listen, understand, and then express words in meaningful contexts.

I Like You, Too

Miguel and María are seated at a table in the classroom eating their lunches. María is playing with a doll. She seems to be more interested in the doll than in her lunch. Miguel, however, appears to be relishing every bite. Miguel begins to contemplate the remainder of his lunch as if trying to decide what to devour next, the apple or the cookies. He picks up a cookie and gets ready to take a bite when he pauses to examine the cookie closely and suddenly exclaims, "I like cookies," smiles, and looks at María expectantly. María, at first, doesn't respond. Miguel repeats, "I like cookies." At this point, María understands Miguel's intent to play a game, looks down at the candy bar on the table, and says, "I like candy." This begins the pattern practice strategy of "Follow the Phrase"—a game to the children.

Miguel: I like cookies.
Miguel: I like cookies.
María: I like candy.
Miguel: I like trucks.
María: I like dolls.
Miguel: I like baseballs.
María: I like jump ropes.
Miguel: I like crayons.
María: I like books.
Miguel: I like you.
María: I like you, too.

PATTERN PRACTICE STRATEGY AND SECOND-LANGUAGE LEARNING
FOLLOW THE PHRASE

"I like you, too." This is the last in a series of statements that seem to be constructed one upon another in a game-like manner. Miguel and María, by repeating the phrase, "I like" with various end tags, are using what appears to be pattern practice as a natural learning strategy to master the grammatical structures of the English language. This strategy is referred to as **Follow the Phrase.**

The strategy, Follow the Phrase, allows Miguel and María to practice the patterns of the second language by keeping constant one part of the sentence, the phrase, and varying the pattern simply by changing the word(s) that follow the phrase. Carroll (1960) states that pattern practice gives drill in the conscious application, variation, and transformation of structural patterns in language, with a view toward making such patterns automatically accessible in actual use of language. Miguel and María, employing the strategy, use patterned phrases as the building blocks of language. The patterns become the basis for communication and can be used to generalize by analogy to parallel linguistic forms and functions.

Carroll suggests that children come to generalize about linguistic structures only after extensive usage of language patterns in a purely repetitive form in real-life communication situations. Elkind (1967) says the repetitive behavior children use is frequently the outward manifestation of an emerging cognitive ability and the need to realize the ability through action. For Miguel and María, the emerging cognitive ability is the facility to communicate in a second language. They use the strategy of Follow the Phrase as the process. This process provides for the repetition and practice of linguistic forms which they must master to be able to communicate in the second language. The intensity of practice exercised by Miguel and María through the strategy may be linked to another fundamental and well-established principle of learning— we learn what we practice. Miguel and María seem to be naturally applying this principle to learning a second language through their use of redundant sequencing of sentences in a game-like manner.

The Follow the Phrase strategy is effective as a learning process because of the elements of redundancy, sequencing, and game-like attributes. First, it utilizes repetitive patterns of phrases. Secondly, it connects these patterns in a topic-comment sequence. Finally, learning proceeds in a game-like fashion. The topic around which Miguel and María modeled their dialogue can be titled, "Things I Like." The patterned phrase, "I like," related their sentences to this theme and permitted Miguel and María to comment on the things they liked by tying the names of their favorite things to the phrase.

Keenan (1976) affirms that topic-comment repetitive sequences are a convention adopted by young children to sustain dialogue. Keenan suggests that the children's use of repetition as the chief means for maintaining topic-comment sequences not only reflects their limited linguistic ability, but also reveals the children's cognizance of their limitations. Therefore, it may be said that Miguel and María, being aware of their limited knowledge of English, use the Follow the Phrase strategy to sustain a dialogue. The redundancy of the initial phrase enables them to communicate in English despite their inexperience with grammar rules and their limited vocabulary. The phrase provides the semantic continuity. Exchanges within the sequence are linked further by a common theme. Brenneis and Lein (1978) state that topic-comment sequences used by children are short and repetitive content exchanges that are tied to a theme and to the form that initiated them. The authors note that these sequences are so tied to the beginning form that failure of one child to respond with the same form terminates the sequence. Thus, María could have terminated the topic-comment sequence begun by Miguel at any point by not responding with the phrase, "I like." It can be noted here that Miguel had difficulty starting the sequence exchange with María and repeated the initial sentence, "I like cookies," twice in order to get the interaction going. Once the interaction began, the semantic continuity of the sequence was maintained by the children's simple repetition of the phrase. The use of the initial phrase also made it possible for the children to anticipate the responses of each other, thus giving them the confidence to use the second language in a playful, game-like way.

Holden and MacGinitie (1972) indicate playful linguistic responses are likely to be redundantly marked. These authors observed the interactive play of children learning a first language and found interactive play with language tended to be repetitive and predictably structured. Garvey (1973) describes patterns of language play where partners alternate exchanges as marked by laughter and perhaps the frivolous rather than serious manner that identifies the whole event. Turn-taking patterns are typical of play. In play situations, each partner shares a key—in this case, the language pattern. This key becomes the stimulus that allows children to chain response sequences through a mode where one child's statement becomes the stimulus for the other child to respond similarly. Miguel, as initiator, started the game of Follow the Phrase by saying "I like cookies." María followed with the statement, "I like candy." Thus, both were drawn into a play situation sharing the phrase "I like" as the key to the topic-sequence interaction. The conversation was characterized by the playful way the children responded to each other. Miguel's statement, "I like you," and his gesture of a bear hug are complemented by María's response, "I like you, too," said with a little smile, confirming the lightheartedness of the exchange.

Ervin-Tripp (1977) states that these verbal-play sequences of discourse with repetition and little variation are believed to contribute to the child's developing mastery of the structures of language. Watson (1975) also sees specific language play routines as important early components of the more developed narrative structures of later years. Researchers of first and second language acquisition have found that children use patterned practice play to learn linguistic structures, both alone in monologues and in dialogues like that of Miguel and María. All sequences of patterns reported by observers, however, can be noted to have the three elements of the Follow the Phrase strategy. One phrase is repeated in a topic-sequence, game-like or playful situation.

Britton (1970) reports the repetitive patterned responses of a girl learning English as a first language. This monologue was said in a sing-song manner as a running commentary on the picture she was drawing—

Draw a nose.
Draw a mouth.
Draw a hat.
Draw a coat.
Draw a shoe.
Draw a dress.
Draw a cat.

Here the phrase, "Draw a," was repeated and sentences were changed by adding ending words of the same grammatical category. The topic is clear from the fact that the commentary is related to the action of drawing the picture. The sing-song manner in which the words are said makes it clear that the words are being said playfully.

Weir (1962) described her son Anthony's monologues as seemingly indefatigable practice of linguistic structures. Anthony systematically used phrases in various topic-sequences to learn his first language, as in the following sequence:

What color mop?
What color glass?
What color chair?
What color truck?
What color table?

Weir remarked that Anthony chimed the words in such a way as to lead the listener to believe he was having fun with the language. Anthony, indeed, was probably having fun while playing without a partner and using the Follow the Phrase strategy as a game. Weir made a point of the fact that children's sequences of utterances, chained by phonological, grammatical or semantic links, often simultaneously, show the associational linking of all three levels of language structure.

Keenan (1976) characterized the dialogue of her twins as being repetitive patterns having one phrase which initiated the exchange and which was repeated in the partner's response. Scotton and Ury (1977) also observed that repetitions in patterned responses were used in an attempt to establish dialogues around topic-sequences for both first and second language learners.

Fillmore's (1980) studies on the language learning strategies of second-language learners include what she terms "pattern practice formulas" which children use in a playful, drill-like way to develop proficiency in the second language. Some samples of the pattern practice which Fillmore observed in bilingual classes in California are:

Kim (Chinese Bilingual Class)

> Gip me raser, Yah!
> Gip me pencil, Yah!
> Gip me chopstick, No!
> Gip me crayon, Yah!
> Gip me paper, Yah!

Tony (Spanish Bilingual)

> What is this? This is a baseball.
> What is that? That is a robin.
> What is that? That is a telephone.
>   etc., for 33 turns, including—
> What is that? That is a you.
> What is that? That is a alphabet.

Miguel and María (also Spanish Bilingual)

Miguel:	María:
Where is the dog?	Here it is.
Where is the cats?	Here it is.
Where is the paper?	Here it is.
Where is the book?	Here it is.

Each of these examples manifests second-language learners' attempting to learn linguistic structures by repeating patterns in topic-comment sequences through verbal play (Follow the Phrase). Tony, in the previous example, had a dialogue with himself. He both asked and answered the questions. The phrase, "that is a," was not varied, however, even when placed in front of the word "alphabet," which would correctly take "an"—another example that illustrates how the phrase is repeated in an unvaried pattern (as a chunk) unchanged by the words which follow. Miguel used the phrase, "Where is the," with cats and María answered, "Here it is." The verb "is" was not changed in the phrase to agree with the noun "cats." Thus, phrases are practiced holistically at first, with attention concentrated on the phrase rather than on the agreement with the tag that follows. The preoccupation with the phrase, practiced in an entertaining repetitive progression, is evidenced by the Chinese girl's mono-logue with "Gip me" as she says "yah" or "no" according to whether or not she has obtained the object requested.

Hakuta (1975) studied a five-year old Japanese girl acquiring English as a second language. He found that the girl, Uguisu, operated within the simple learning system of pattern practice to initially learn the language. Hatch (1978) comments on recent research on discourse analysis which suggests that second-language learners internalize language rules on the basis of practice of patterns acquired in discourse sets.

The research on first and second language acquisition, therefore, sub-stantiates the statement that children use topic-sequenced pattern practice in a game-like mode to learn ordered sequences of words. The dialogues of Miguel and María are consistent with the researchers' findings. The Follow the Phrase strategy allows children to try out language patterns in close connection with their immediate environment in a meaningful way. Simple patterns practiced and expressed in relevant descriptive statements launch the learner into social discourse in the language. As more patterns are learned, children begin to combine the patterns in more complex ways. Thus, in due time, Miguel's statement "I like you" to María can become, "I like you, but I have other friends, too."

IMPLICATIONS OF FOLLOW THE PHRASE FOR SECOND-LANGUAGE LEARNING AND CLASSROOM TEACHING

Children learning a second language naturally adopt the strategy of Follow the Phrase to practice word patterns. This fact can be taken as support for the popular teaching technique of teaching second language through patterned oral drills. These procedures are justified on the basis of theories and observations as to how children learn a second language and how they function in drawing upon the well-practiced patterns on a purely oral level to impart information. It may be true that the pattern practice procedure matches the children's natural learning strategy in theory, but in application the traditional teaching method of patterned practice fails to conform to the way children learn language patterns because it leaves out the most important factor—meaning. Children learn patterns which are meaningful to them and can be applied in a social context. Conversely, most pattern practice taught in second-language drills fails to provide meaning to the patterns students practice. Students are expected to memorize long drills of sentences and practice using them in the precise form memorized. Rivers (1980) terms this type of drill "mindless pattern practicing." Students learn patterns as part of a rote, tedious, mechanistic process where they do not make any personal contribution. Rivers points out that one of the dangers of this type of practice is that students often make errors when they begin to extend by analogy the use of structures that have been practiced in a mechanical, unthinking manner with little meaning. Jarvis (1980) gives an example that further elucidates the meaningless pattern practice often observed in classrooms.

> One can observe classes where students repeat patterns such as, "I don't like blue jeans, I don't like . . . ," etc., but one never knows whether the students did or did not like blue jeans. Usually, the student was only making the sounds of the words because the drill or exercise required the making of them. Sometimes the exercises looked very much like communication, but when one saw the bored expressions on the children's faces one knew it was only a semblance of communication—that carried no meaning for the learner.

In the classrooms, Jarvis describes practice patterns that include random sets of grammatically correct but unrelated statements. In these classrooms, children like Miguel and María would not be encouraged to generate a patterned sequence of exchanges from the phrase, "I like." They would be told exactly *what* to say they liked. Miguel and María would repeat, "I like liver; I like Texas," etc., and whether they liked liver or Texas would be as unimportant to the lesson format as the weather outside the classroom.

It is apparent that this type of pattern practice is not the same as that practiced by children naturally. Children relate patterns to relevant topic-comment sequences, often in social interactions. Halliday (1970) says relating patterns to a meaningful social context enables speakers to construct connected passages of discourse that are situationally relevant. Relevance and meaning, then, are components that facilitate the successful learning of language patterns; pattern practice without these components is, more often than not, unsuccessful in teaching linguistic patterns that transfer to natural communication. Miguel and María's natural pattern practice was obviously germane since they used the phrase "I like" to comment on their favorite things and finally related it to their feelings about each other. The question is, then, how can teachers remodel pattern practice drills to reflect the natural way children use this strategy to learn a second language?

Rivers (1980) encourages teachers to regard pattern practice as a tool for teaching children to experiment creatively with the small amount of language they have acquired. Teachers must provide more opportunities for spontaneous generation of patterns by the children. Teachers can begin this process by integrating the three elements that comprise the natural way children learn language patterns into a lesson format. First, phrases are repeated. Secondly, they are tied to a topic. Finally, they are practiced in a game-like situation. The teacher may proceed in the following way:

1. Generate topic-sequences based on students' interests. For example: Places I go, People I know, Things I play with, Foods I eat, etc.

2. Ask a question to initiate the topic—What do you eat? Teach students a phrase—"I eat."

3. Translate the phrase once for further clarification.

4. Use the phrase in a contextually relevant manner, using concrete objects or pictures. If the phrase is "I eat," the teacher holds up a number of foods or pictures of foods and says, "I eat carrots; I eat meat, etc." (Peabody Picture Cards © have excellent pictures.) The teacher also could present real fruits and vegetables.

5. Review and teach the names of foods with the children as a group, repeating the phrase, "I eat" with the name of each food. "I eat grapes. I eat . . . ," etc.

6. Play the game-like strategy, Follow the Phrase, by lining up pictures of food, or real food, in front of the class. Each child chooses a food he or she likes and then repeats the phrase, "I eat." The next child follows the phrase by choosing another favorite food and says, "I eat . . . ." When it is again the first child's turn, he or she chooses another picture of a food. The child says "I eat grapes," and restates the phrase with the first card chosen—"I eat grapes; I eat apples." Thus, a child eventually is saying a sequence of sentences using the phrase "I eat" to comment upon the chosen group of foods.

> I eat grapes.
> I eat meat.
> I eat tomatoes, etc.

A follow-up activity might be for children to find pictures of foods they like in magazines, to cut out, and comment upon.

7. Allow children to use phrases creatively. When a number of phrases have been learned, encourage children to initiate the game by providing the phrase that is the impetus for the pattern practice of the group. Other topics for Follow the Phrase are storybook characters and TV characters. The teacher talks about the characters, thereby setting the topic. A question-answer drill is used to initiate the pattern practice.

Teacher: What's his/her name? (Shows picture of TV character)

His/her name is . . .   (Teacher models phrases children are to reply with)

Student: His name is Fonzie.

Students choose a picture of the TV or storybook characters they want to name in response to the teacher's question—"What's his/her name?"

Students accumulate a number of pictures and practice the pattern, "His/her name is . . ." by saying in sequence the names of people in all the pictures they have.

His name is Fonzie.
His name is Archie.
His name is Charlie Brown, etc.

Initially, it may be best to have children learn all male or all female characters. Later, the phrases "His name is" and "Her name is" can be intermingled.

8. Another variation of the strategy is to use the theme of a class store. The teacher and students collect items for a class store. Students learn the names for items. The topic posed then could be: Things I want from the store. The teacher asks the question, "What do you want from the store?" Children respond by saying, "I want . . . ," and pick up the object. Again, a sequence of statements to match objects chosen is reiterated turn-after-turn.

These activities are just a few of the ways the teacher can use the Follow the Phrase strategy in a game-like situation to teach children patterns of the second language. The teacher, in fact, can utilize all four types of pattern-practice drills (repetition, chain, substitution, and question-answer) to construct activities for students which relate pattern practice to meaningful statements that make it possible for children to comment upon their world.

Monane (1980) emphasizes teaching meaningful patterns to students that conform to the socio-semantic contexts of everyday life. She calls the drills she has devised "Production Drills." Production drills include: gossip patterns, bragging patterns, and information-seeking patterns. Language patterns are taught with these topics which allow students to learn effective ways to communicate in social contexts.

Troike (1974) advocates teaching language patterns through songs. Many songs require the repetition of phrases. For example, "Here We Go Around the Mulberry Bush" is a song where the phrase, "This is the way we . . . ," is repeated over and over. Children are free to add different endings.

Another type of pattern practice is called the box drill. This type of drill is utilized in the game "What's Happening?" First, children decide on a social event such as a picnic, party, dance, etc. On the board the teacher writes:

Who   What   Where

Children give names of people who are at a picnic and what they are doing. The pattern of language is used for "Where" the action is taking place such as, on the grass; in the boat; etc. The "What" part of the box can also be used for teaching patterns such as present progressive "is sleeping" etc. "What" and

"Where" boxes are thus programmed for pattern practice. Pattern practice for the present progressive is seen in the following example:

Who	What	Where
María	is sleeping	in the boat.
John	is running	on the grass.
Miguel	is riding	in the car.

Sentences are stated initially going across, such as "María is sleeping in the boat." Then they are combined into new patterns, such as "María is running in the boat" and "John is sleeping in the car." Children enjoy this type of drill because of the many humorous ways sentences can be recombined.

Each of these language lessons builds on the natural learning strategy of children and their propensity to Follow the Phrase. Lessons use repetition in topic-centered sequences to teach relevant language patterns in a game-like situation. Patterns taught are relevant because they involve students in communicating about their feelings, values and world. Relevant patterns learned are easily transferred to new social contexts.

Pattern practice as a teaching strategy also has value in that it enables the teacher to use language in drills to present new linguistic elements in an ordered sequence. The more language can be reduced to consistent patterns at first, the more easily it can be transferred to verbal interactions. The learning of a language is an exceedingly complex task, yet children seem to learn language naturally by unconsciously applying various strategies that enable them to derive meaning from the spoken word while practicing linguistic structures. The strategy of Follow the Phrase is one where children repeat language patterns. The teacher can reinforce this strategy by designing game activities that make it possible for children to follow phrase, after phrase, after phrase—an unerring path down the road to second-language fluency.

Gimme the Sweetie

Cinco de Mayo is being celebrated with a grand fiesta by the students at the school. Parents have been invited to attend a performance of song and dance put on by the children. After the class presentation, parents, students, and the teacher gather at several round tables to "socialize" and partake of cakes, Mexican sweetbreads, ice cream, coffee, and soda. The teacher, with the aid of the students, has set each table very formally with a white tablecloth, colorful napkins, china cups, a china coffeepot, creamer, and sugar bowl. Cordiality and social greetings pervade the classroom. Parents and students seat them-selves rather formally at the tables for refreshments and to converse. One small group of students, however, in the corner of the classroom, is socializing in an uproarious, informal manner. The teacher decides to join this group. As the teacher sits down with the group, the tenor of the socializing changes instantaneously, both linguistically and behaviorally. Language forms reflect formal politeness; behavior becomes very sedate and proper.

Miguel: Hey, man! How you doing?

Carlos: Cool, man!

María   Gimme the sweetie! (Miguel grabs sugar from the bowl and flips it in the air.)

Rosa: Stop it! Look out! Don't, silly! I'm gonna tell!

Miguel: Hey, Carlos! Wanna play?

Carlos: Lemme have the sweetie!

Miguel: (Flipping the sugar.) There you go—right there! (Points under the table.)

Carlos: (Goes under the table.)

Miguel: How you doing?

Carlos: Gonna get some more.

Miguel: (Throwing the sugar.) Over there—You gotta hurry up!

Teacher: (Joins group.) I'm going to sit here and have a cup of coffee with you. María, please pass the sugar. Thank you.

Carlos: May I have some soda?

María: Please pass the sugar.

Teacher: Say thank you.

María: Thank you.

Teacher: Good afternoon, Miguel. How are you?

Miguel: (Turns away from the table, looking bored.)

Teacher: Good afternoon, Miguel. How are you?

Miguel: Good afternoon, Mrs. Baca. How are you?

Teacher: Have you enjoyed the party?

Miguel: May I please go out to play?

FORMAL-INFORMAL STYLE SOCIAL RELATIONS STRATEGY AND SECOND-LANGUAGE LEARNING
SOCIALIZING

María asks for sugar in two distinctly different ways in the preceding conversations: "Gimme the sweetie!" and "Please pass the sugar." Both of these requests are meaningful in the social context in which they are embedded. The expressions communicate the same request but the words have been appropriately matched to the informal group and to the formal group social interactions. María has learned these social formulas in communication contexts with peers and with the teacher, and she has derived a similar meaning in each instance by observing how the expressions related to the ongoing activities or the social interaction. Once these social formulas have become familiar to María, she can use them holistically in other similar social settings as a strategy to communicate in the second language. The strategy of imitating expressions heard in social exchanges and applying them to other appropriate social settings is termed **Socializing.**

Second-language acquisition can be thought of in this strategy as the child's development of productive control over the language system as an outcome of dynamic social discourse. From this perspective, language is used to serve social ends and social relationships. Socializing can be regarded as an accommodating strategy. Language learned through interaction is modified by the situation. Through a series of conversations in different contexts, the child becomes a productive user of speech. Productive use of language, that is, control over grammatical structure and reference systems, arises almost as a by-product of social discourse (Harris 1975).

Students learn to initiate conversations by Socializing with such attention-getters as, "Hi!" "Excuse me," and "How you doing?" Students utilize the strategy of Socializing to make and maintain relationships with speakers of the target language in order to receive necessary input in the language. Fillmore (1976) states:

> A language cannot be learned without input, and to get input of the right sort the learner needs exposure to the language as it is used in social situations which involve him. . . . The social problem in second-language learning comes down to two major issues—how to get along socially without a common language, and how to get your friends to want to help you learn theirs. Obviously, this means that the learner must want to be part of the social group that speaks the language. Typically, the learner is motivated not so much to learn the language as to become part of the social world of its speakers.

According to Fillmore, the Socializing strategy taps the resource of one's friends in social conversations, with the by-product being language learning. The establishment of social relations is thus an important part of second-language learning. The social relation components which are essential to the development of a second language include:

1. Social interaction.
2. Establishing and maintaining social relationships through the use of expressions or formulas.
3. Learning informal and formal usages of language.
4. Receiving feedback from the teacher and peers.
5. Possessing social skills which assist in language learning.

The *first* essential social relations component that develops in second language is manifested by the following social axiom, "Join a group and act as if you understand what is going on, even if you don't." (Fillmore 1976). This axiom implies that it is up to the second-language learner as an "outsider" to invite interaction with peers in order to be accepted as part of the social group. Once they are members of the group, they learn the second language as a result of the social process of working and playing with target language speakers. Knowledge of the second language is gained as children practice using English in social interactions. The more interactions that take place, the more practice is said to have occurred. Seliger (1977) did a study to test the hypothesis that learners who practice initiating interactions and thereby cause a concomitant input from others will benefit more from practice opportunities. Seliger labeled children who initiated interactions and socialized intensively with peers as "high input generators." "Low input generators," on the other hand, interacted infrequently with peers. Seliger found that high input generators did, in fact, benefit more from practice opportunities and thus learned language better and faster. Seliger concludes that the natural behavior of interacting with native language speakers may be one of the most important strategies in the language acquisition process.

Children learn the second language naturally through spontaneous social interaction. Hymes (1971) states that the language children attend to and learn from others significant in their environment is addressed to them in "spontaneous, but highly social interactions." As children attend to these social interactions and gradually participate in them, they learn what Hymes calls "communicative competence." Communicative competence has two aspects. It includes both knowledge of the language and knowledge of the social world. These aspects of communicative competence are realized in children's actual speech behavior or performance in conversations.

The second language (like a first language) evolves and develops as children learn to carry on a conversation. Conversational activity enables second-language learners to comprehend the dynamic meaning of language through a shared reference system which allows them to communicate with words whose meaning is shared by intimate members of the peer social group (Peirce 1932). María's directive to Miguel, "Gimme the sweetie!" resulted in Miguel's throwing her a sugar cube. This interaction could take place because the children shared the meaning of "sweetie." The meaning of the word was gleaned by María from the social context. As children learn a language through conversations in social contexts, they learn what uses of language are possible and appropriate and tailor the usage to fit the context.

Establishing and maintaining social relationships or friendships with native speakers through the use of social expressions or formulas is the *second* social relations component important to second-language development. Pinnell (1975) found in studying children's language in the classroom that about half of the language she recorded could be classified as "interactional" in the sense that it was used to build and maintain social relationships. Pinnell states:

> Children made statements such as, "Let's work in the sand," "Trade you two of these for one of those." Through language interactions with peers, they had a chance to practice cooperation and develop social skills. Children constantly engaged in interactional language, using language as the critical tool to facilitate the maintenance of social relationships.

Cohen (1975) notes that by socializing, children learn to adapt their speech to match that of those around them. Garvey and Hogan (1973) label this "social speech," or speech strictly modeled to that of peers. Hornby (1977) speaks of social exchange patterns or expressions children use in order to be part of the social group. Expressions such as "sweetie" and "Cool, man" are in-group expressions that second-language learners pick up to establish their social identity with the group, as well as to learn the target language. Hatch (1972) refers to social expressions used with peers, such as "Get out of here," as being the first to be acquired with full comprehension by second-language learners. These expressions are learned as the by-product of social communicative needs.

Social expressions are generally linguistic formulas which are highly context-specific and can be learned and used by children even though they know nothing about the internal structure of the language. In general, they are used as invariant forms. Once students master these formulas, however, they can socialize more easily. These social formulas also have been referred to as "routines." Hymes (1972) has defined linguistic routines as "sequences of verbal behavior." He states that they constitute "organizations beyond the sentence." A "communicative routine" may be thought of as a sequence of utterances or behaviors which is regular and procedural and which communicates as much by form as by content. Verbal routines that occur in conversations include: greetings, shouts, and verbal play (Ervin-Tripp 1977). Routines are learned informally through contextually based communication with peers as part of the peer-group vernacular and later are used by second-language learners to structure a large part of discourse (Watson 1975). The expressions that Miguel and María used in the peer-group conversation that are clearly social routines include: "Wait a minute!" "Here you go," and "How you doing?"

Routines or social formulas also are learned from adults. Formal social formulas acquired from adults are marked from the beginning and treated differently from other language behavior. One factor that sets routines apart from the other language taught to children by adults is the general failure of adults to provide explanations or expansions based on them. Politeness routines and greetings, such as "How are you?" "Fine," and "Thanks," do not spark any explanation such as that found in adults' teaching of lexical items. Routines provide the means for children to make moves in social interactions (Boggs and Watson-Gegeo 1978). Children learn formal routines through conversation and instruction from the teacher in the classroom. These formal routines include: polite requests, polite refusals, and how to initiate and end a social encounter.

The acquisition of social formulas or routines is important for second-language learners because through the use of routines children can communicate in the second language almost immediately. The acquisition of these formulas, however, proceeds in the opposite direction from much of the rest of language. Generally, competence in language comes first, then performance—language is mapped onto some prior cognition. With routines, performance comes first. Children learning a second language use these routines holistically to socialize before they understand the rules of syntax that make the construction of these routines possible. Syntactic knowledge, however, is not the goal of second-language learners. Their goal is to establish social relations with peers and with adult speakers of the second language. By doing this, they inadvertently learn the new language as a natural component in the socializing process.

The *third* essential social relations component in mastering a second language includes socializing in both formal and informal situations. Major sources of input and modeling for second-language learners in the school setting are the teacher and peers. Teachers usually communicate with formal language, while peers rely on informal, casual speech. By socializing in an informal situation with peers, students learn a casual or vernacular speech style. Labov (1972) defines casual speech as "the everyday speech used in informal settings when no attention is directed to language." Second-language learners get a feel for the target language by not having to concentrate on grammatical rules. Attention is concentrated instead on "getting a message across" in an intimate, personal setting. Collaborative patterns predominate. Shared words, slang expressions, fragmentary responses, and contradictions are very common. Expressions used by Miguel and María in their conversations with peers may, in fact, be characterized as phrases and fragmentary responses. Expressions to peers included: "Stop it," "There you go," and "Look out." Peer social exchanges provide students with reciprocal social experience, trial and error with language forms in a non-authoritarian atmosphere, and positive peer reinforcement.

The importance of social interactions with peers in an informal setting for second-language development has been alluded to by many authors (Hartup 1977). Students have been noted to engage in one hundred interpersonal exchanges a day with peers (Grant 1979). Informal involvement with peers can vary along several lines—affiliation, social intimacy, cooperation, and competition. Regardless of the involvement children have with each other, they are being socialized in the informal use of the second language.

The formal speech style is learned by children chiefly through educational socialization. School is a socially significant phenomenon which triggers a language switch from informal peer vernacular to the formal language appropriate to the educational domain (DeStefano and Rental 1975). The main communicative function in the traditional classroom is the transmission of knowledge from a teacher who knows formal language usage to pupils who do not (Furlong and Edwards 1977). It has become increasingly apparent that children's language acquisition is facilitated by the specialized input from adults around them. In conversations with an adult, children are likely to accept the pattern of interaction set by the adult and reciprocate with discourse structured in the same formal manner. Miguel responds to the teacher's formal greeting, "Good afternoon, Mrs. Baca. How are you?" This type of full-echo response is often observed in social responses of students with teachers. Miguel's formal social greeting to the teacher is in direct contrast to the informal greeting he used with his peer, Carlos—"How you doing?"

Another distinction between formal and informal speech is that instructional elements often appear in adult speech, whereas informal speech interactions are more conducive to malleable, collaborative roles and are subject to transformations by the activity changes. The instructional element in formal speech between adult and child is often designated by authoritative markers such as, "Say." In the formal conversation between the teacher and the students, the teacher tells María to "Say, 'thank you.'" María responds by repeating, "Thank you." Markers are used particularly by adults in teaching formal, polite speech. A study by Gleason and Weintraub (1976) on the acquisition of politeness formulas claims that these expressions are acquired differently from the rest of language. The authors believe that politeness formulas are explicitly taught to children by parents or teachers who prompt their use with markers such as, "Say," or "What do you say?" These politeness formulas or routines have little structure or variability and are learned as appropriate for a situation rather than to express a referential meaning.

All speakers of a language, whether it is their first or second, are bound by the constraints of appropriateness and politeness in formal settings (Holmes and Brown 1976). Children become aware that they must use "please" and "thank you" when requesting something formally from an adult, while they may use simple imperatives to peers. Miguel prefaces his request to the teacher with, "May I please?" He is aware that direct requests cannot be made in the formal setting with the teacher. When interacting with Carlos in informal conversation, Miguel issues the simple imperative—"You gotta hurry up." The focus of the request shifts from polite solicitation to emphasis on the action. Hollos and Beeman (1978) studied directives given by Norwegian and Hungarian children to adults and peers. Both Norwegian and Hungarian children were aware of the social division between adults and peers, and changed their language accordingly. Directives to peers were more informal, with directional shifts in the focus according to who was addressed, for the action that was to be carried out. A directive such as, "Run over there," may be said to a peer. The use of the directive here implies that the speaker has the authority to compel the hearer to act.

A variety of formal interpersonal social formulas are learned from the teacher, such as greetings and leave-takings. These politeness formulas, according to Goffman (1971), are among the most conventionalized language forms used in social activities. Once these formulas have been internalized by students, a given formula triggers an automatic response. Thus, "How are you?" is responded to with the formula, "Fine." The development of social polite formulas gives second-language learners a social sensitivity. Students become very sensitive to social influences and acquire formal language in direct correspondence to specific adult linguistic standards (Hollos and Beeman 1978).

Second-language learners must learn not only social interaction formulas and vocabulary of both formal and informal language, but also must develop role behavior to match the style of language to different social settings. They must learn to behave linguistically in all the culturally determined roles which the language recognizes: to ask and answer questions, to respond to commands, to vary the key of utterances, and to explore the range of linguistic relations (Levine 1976). Halliday (1968) explains, "Language is a form of culturally determined behavior and this behavior includes the ability to take on a range of linguistically defined roles in speech situations." Hymes (1967) and Houston (1969) report some of the primary situational determinants that enable students to accomplish this linguistic matching as: participants, tone, purpose, scene, and key.

Miguel and María employ these situational determinants to match their linguistic style to the informal conversation with their peers, and then to the formal conversation with the teacher, at the Cinco de Mayo celebration. In considering the form of correct language usage, Miguel first appraises the participants in the informal group who are all his social equals. Thus, he uses an informal style of language with shared group expressions, such as, "Cool, man!" María also considers the participants in the group in her use of the word "sweetie." While the word "sweetie" can be used appropriately by María in the interaction with her peers, it is not appropriate for use in the more formal situation with the teacher; here the word "sugar" is correct and fits the more formal situation. In fact, the word "sweetie" not only is inappropriate in the formal situation but it also may not carry the same meaning; the teacher, hearing the word, may think of it as a term of endearment if she knows nothing of the peer-group vernacular. María has come to understand what Levine (1976) terms "goodness of fit." Vocabulary usage is tied directly to the participants in the group to whom it will be expressed. Labov (1972) states that the more a way of speaking becomes shared and meaningful within a group, the more likely the meaning will be shared only among group members, or be what Labov terms "context bound."

Another situational variant that Miguel and María use as a clue to match their language style to the setting is the tone of the interaction. Tone is roughly equivalent to social attitude (Levine 1976). When the teacher joins the peer group, the tone of the linguistic and behavioral interaction changes immediately. It no longer is appropriate to be personal or intimate. The throwing of sugar cubes stops. The group becomes sedate. Miguel sits on his chair, as does Carlos. The teacher conveys a social distance which elicits this behavior on the part of the children. Waller (1967) writes:

> Social distance is characteristic of the personal entanglements of teachers and students. It is necessary where the subordination of one person to another is required, for distance makes possible that recession of feeling without which the authority of another is intolerable.

The children perceive the teacher's role as a socially distant one and adjust their language appropriately to follow the teacher's lead. The teacher, in fact, does lead the conversation and maintains the formality of the interaction with the children by adopting what Ferguson (1974) describes as "teaching language." The teacher initiates questions. She uses children's names as attention-getting devices to teach polite expressions such as, "María, say thank-you." She uses repetitions and utterances in the interrogative form. She asks Miguel, "Have you enjoyed the party?" Reciprocity with the teacher is maintained by the students through a balance of imitation and response routines. María imitates the teacher's statement, "Please pass the sugar." Miguel gives back an exact copy to the teacher of her greeting routine, "Good afternoon." This formality in tone is achieved through precise structured discourse. All responses are given in complete sentences. Only a minority of the utterances relate to ongoing activity or are contextually oriented. There is a definite formal structure imposed on the tone of the conversation as a result of the teacher's presence in the group. Hymes (1964) explains the change in tone by pointing out that any time children speak to others outside their intimate group there is the likelihood that they will pay more attention to speech than when interacting with peers.

The tone in the informal group with peers is one of mutual playfulness. The language of discourse reflects the lightness of the interaction. Language is characterized by the use of phrases. Children issue commands to each other such as, "Stop it!" There is a mutual sharing of conversation direction. Direction of the conversation is not set as in the formal setting but flows with the ongoing activity.

The purpose of the social interaction also has an effect on language usage and role behavior. Purpose is defined as the outcome or goal of the situation (Hymes 1967). The goal of the informal conversation in the peer group is to set up a play situation and to use language to communicate what is occurring. Communication is natural and relates directly to play. The fact that the focus of the interaction is on play is clearly expressed in Miguel's probe to Carlos, "Wanna play?"

When the teacher joins the group the purpose of the interaction changes. The formally set table becomes the focus for the teacher to instruct the children in good manners. The teacher functions as a socializing agent by formally giving lessons in proper linguistic and social etiquette.

The last of the situational variables that influence communicative interaction are scene and key. The scene refers to the psychological setting (Hymes 1967). The key is the manner or spirit in which something is said or done. The same setting with different people may redefine the interaction. The use of language may change from informal to formal (Hymes 1967). The key in this particular conversation went from unrestrained to restrained upon the teacher's arrival in the group. This switch in key was noted as the spontaneity went out of the children's conversation. The change from playfulness to formality was so intense that Miguel pleads with the teacher for a change of key by saying, "May I please go out to play?" Miguel recognizes that the formal interaction with the teacher can no longer be defined as a play setting.

By applying situational determinants, Miguel and María can better match their language to the rules of etiquette of formal language and to the vernacular of informal peer language. The children become aware that even when the content of what is being said remains constant, people speak differently in formal and informal conversations. Situational determinants to social encounters are inferred regularities in the interaction patterns in formal and informal settings upon which the children will base their expectancies for correct language usage for future similar encounters. Sachs and Devin (1976) and Feldman (1974) did studies of children talking to adults and peers to measure children's responsiveness to situational social cues. Children were noted to have different speech styles for adults and peers. This research reveals that "knowing a style might be thought of as a shortcut to learning language successfully as a social tool."

The *fourth* social relations component essential to second-language learning is feedback from the teacher and peers. Feedback that children receive from the teacher in formal situations is characterized by repetition, rule isolation, and verification of correct form. Teachers supplement children's linguistic knowledge in a definite, conscious way through direct instruction. They model proper grammatical forms and then ask children to repeat them. They monitor children's speech to isolate rules that children are noted to need to practice and devise dialogues or instructional events where practice can occur (Krashen 1976). Finally, they correct ungrammatical usage and verify proper form by verbal positive reinforcement such as, "Good; That's right!"

Peer language feedback is much more subtle. By trying out newly acquired language in natural social encounters, second-language learners come to understand implicitly what language forms best fit various interactions. They shape their language to the responses they receive from peers. Feedback is often given in the context of a game. Children use social formulas to gain access to and participate in the game. Feedback from peers is the acknowledgement of their correct selection of social formulas by allowing them to participate. Fillmore (1976) states that peers also provide direct feedback for second-language learners. She notes in her study of second-language learners that peers helped each other by correcting their utterances from time to time.

> Peers occasionally rephrased and repeated the learners' sentences by way of verifying their own interpretations. Corrections were never structural; it seems peers were able to accept gross problems with structure without comment. Most important was content. Peers gave feedback to interpret correctly what second-language learners were trying to say.

Feedback from peers concerns how well a message is conveyed in the sense that it is understandable. Teacher feedback, contrarily, is given to underscore grammatical or structural correctness of a statement.

The facile development of second language may be regarded as a "pas de deux" between content feedback from peers and structural feedback from the teacher. Children's conversational exchange with peers and with the teacher in varying contexts gives them productive control over the language system both for meaningful discourse and for correct grammatical usage.

The *fifth* essential social relations component which promotes second-language learning is the possession of specific social skills. Second-language learners must possess the social skills which motivate them to socialize with native language speakers even when there is little or no language in common. Tucker (1976) describes social characteristics of successful second-language learners as: "adventuresome, willing to venture out into the target language, peer-centered, assertive, and possessing a positive attitude toward target-language speakers." Gardner (1976) refers to a positive attitude as an "integrative motive." Underlying characteristics of the integrative motive is that it reflects a high level of drive on the part of the child to acquire a valued target language. Fathman (1976) reports that children making the most progress in the second language had social skills which could be characterized as friendly and talkative. Children who are naturally talkative, outgoing, confident, friendly, and desirous of being with other children possess the social skills which enable them to establish relationships with others despite any language barrier.

In summary, it may be said that language and social behavior are related phenomena. Language is an individually differentiated form of behavior determined specifically by the social context in which it is embedded. A second language is not learned independently of social variables but is, in fact, socially situated and socially defined. This means that the social context is the most powerful determinant of verbal behavior (Labov 1970). Children put into practice the strategy of Socializing to gain increased mastery of the new language. The strategy consists of *five* components: social interaction, establishing and maintaining relationships or friendships through the use of social expressions or formulas, learning informal and formal language styles, receiving feedback from peers and teachers, and possessing social skills that promote language learning.

IMPLICATIONS OF SOCIALIZING FOR SECOND-LANGUAGE LEARNING AND CLASSROOM TEACHING

Second-language learning in the school setting will be advanced inasmuch as the classroom is used simultaneously as a formal and informal linguistic environment emphasizing active language use. The informal language is learned from peer interaction. Teacher instruction increases the learner's conscious knowledge of grammatical, formal language. The key to the difference in formal and informal speech usage is the social situation. The classroom teacher, therefore, must build varying language forms into meaningful small-group activities. Baker (1976) provides a completely developed rationale for small-group work as well as for operational procedures and sample small-group activities. He suggests the following guidelines to maximize the possibility that small-group learning will create productive language usage:

1. Students should clearly understand the purpose of a group activity and use language to discuss what they are doing.

2. Each group should have appropriate materials with which to work and be taught their labels in the second language.

3. Students should clearly understand the outcome of each activity so that dialogue is meaningful and related to specified performance objectives.

Language and small-group activity should be tied to specific outcomes and be meaningfully interrelated. Gunderson (1978) suggests that teachers select small-group activities that primarily emphasize communication. By making communication the fundamental goal, the teacher encourages both grammatically correct utterances and the use of spontaneous speech. The goal of small-group activities is to increase students' communicative or stylistic competence, that is, to teach them to handle a wider and wider range of language modifications.

Small-group activities are teacher-mediated in that the teacher sets the goals and objectives. Activities are also peer-mediated, where the students are respondents and informed sources or monitors for each other. Students can work together in small groups on controlled or decontrolled assignments. The group works as a unit to produce a response. The teacher's role is essentially that of a guide, monitor or prescriber. The teacher accepts the spontaneous flow of casual peer language, but also introduces formal language patterns that relate to the task, moving from known to unknown structures. As the teacher moves from group to group, he or she observes and listens to conversations to isolate grammatical forms which may need to be reintroduced in additional small-group teacher-directed language learning sessions.

Small-group activities provide students with opportunities for oral and aural development of the second language. Heterogeneity in groups serves to foster interaction. Those students of lesser ability are learning, while those of greater ability are teaching and using what they have already internalized and now need to practice. Since English is the medium of communication, the group work should stimulate the participants and motivate them toward greater use of English in meaningful contexts.

Units of study may be the focus for group activities. Discussion relates to the topic and reinforces the learning of relevant vocabulary. Kohn (1975) describes unit instruction where students are encouraged to bring to class every day a picture that correlates with the unit under study. Students are then given an opportunity to talk about their pictures. Kohn believes this reinforces the vocabulary learned as part of the unit. Second-language learners quickly pick up new vocabulary words when they are tied to physical tasks. Vocabulary learned as part of the unit then becomes the medium for meaningful exchange of information between learners and their peers.

Games provide another vehicle for Socializing and reinforce the meaningful exchange of information that is so important in second-language learning. Ratner and Bruner (1978) comment on the nature of games that assist children with language learning.

1. Games usually have a restricted format with a limited number of semantic elements.
2. Games have a clear repetitive structure which allows both for anticipation of the order of events and variation of individual elements.

Words used in a game are usually closely tied to the game's actions and thus are more meaningful to the second-language learner. The simplicity of most games sanctions the use of highly repetitive, socially formulaic language. Games in small groups provide language models in a natural setting. Social contact is established and maintained within the shared theme of the game (Martlew 1978). Different norms for language usage defined by interpersonal relations are learned in varying game contexts (Crockenberg et al. 1976). Interpersonal language skills are developed as children communicate in order to play the game.

Ball games and other formally and informally structured sports promote active language usage. Play in a game may be thought of as a social context in which language can be learned as a way of fitting activities together. Language is not learned as an end in itself, but as the means to play and talk about "moves" in the game. Language is spontaneous and action-specific, and therefore has meaning for second-language learners. The strategy of Socializing can naturally be employed by students to learn the language formulas that are socially appropriate to game participation.

Games which have been suggested to aid second-language learning include the "Jigsaw Puzzle Game." Each student in this game has a piece of a puzzle. Children must work together to complete the puzzle, using language to discuss placement of parts. A variation of this game is to use puzzle parts that are part of a scene to be guessed, such as pieces of furniture in a room. Puzzle games also can be matching games. Two teams are selected. Each team has only one-half of a picture. The task is to be able to verbally solicit the other half of the puzzle from opposing team members. Second-language learners may rely on more proficient English speakers on their team to assist them with the vocabulary needed for descriptions. Each child has one turn and can ask only one question per turn. Teams get points for each completed picture.

Richards (1975), in an article on "Singing as a Fun Route to Second-Language Learning," discusses the value of singing games for language learning. Richards states that singing has the advantage of teaching new vocabulary and sentence patterns in a group situation. Songs are repetitive and may be combined with actions to further meaningful language learning.

Curran (1972) describes another method of small-group second-language learning which can be conducted in a game situation. Children sit in two circles, one inside the other. The inner circle is composed of second-language learners. The outer circle consists of children who are bilingual. A box containing some object is placed in the middle of the inner circle. Children take turns guessing what is in the box. Children ask questions to determine the contents of the box. Questions are directed to the outer circle team leader who knows the contents of the box. Children may pose the questions initially in their first language. They then turn around and the bilingual child translates the question into English. Children then repeat the question in English. In spite of all this translation, this method, according to Curran, involves meaningful language practice. This method, along with the other small-group activities previously mentioned, gives students practice in the target language in a game situation which is intrinsically motivating. The impetus to learn the language results from the children's desire to become effective players in the game.

A small-group educational technique suggested by Levin (1977) encourages children to gossip. Levin believes that face-to-face gossip plays an important socializing role and aids second-language learning. Levin cites the *London Times* (1954) as giving support to his claim.

A recommendation has been made that children in schools should be encouraged to gather in small groups for gossip sessions as an aid in learning English is made by the Education Committee Inspectors, who have concluded an inspection of schools throughout the country . . . The inspectors claim that emphasis on oral expression can be achieved by allowing children to talk naturally about things which interest them.

Fine (1977) comments on children's gossip in terms of four components which support second-language learning.

1. content-socialization component
2. normative or evaluative component
3. interpersonal-social structural component
4. ability-competence component

Each of these components acts in concert to make gossip an important interactional tool for children learning a new language. The content-socialization component is one of the most important elements of gossip. It allows for the transfer of information in specific social contexts. Students thus acquire social formulas and phrases that are meaningfully related to social interactions. The evaluative component is closely tied to the factual content of gossip. Most gossip carries explicitly or implicitly some perspective on the behavior being described. Thus, it has been suggested that gossip is one of the chief means by which norms of language for socializing are stated and reaffirmed. Gossip permits children to talk about topics of interest with the result that they become actively involved in communication. Finally, the ability-competence component refers to the language proficiency which is the outcome of learning to gossip well. Abrahams (1979) makes a strong case for the use of gossip as a language-learning device. He affirms that through gossip children can learn the rules of linguistic competence. It is not simply the content of gossip, but the style of speaking which is learned as well. Through gossip children have the opportunity to learn language in a natural context with peers providing examples of speech that are particular to their social world.

A language curriculum can extend children's natural language-learning strategy of Socializing by providing for ongoing, informal, and formal group activities centered around social groups. Halliday (1968) states that language learning is advanced in an environment in which speech situation roles are open to children informally, but are also offered through systematic teaching in formal small-group sessions. The teacher's job is to create opportunities for children to acquire language naturally as they pursue group projects, game activities, or indulge in gossip. To accomplish this goal, teachers must not only use controlled exercises in formal instructional sessions, but must also allow for decontrolled activities which are part of natural peer-group interaction. Students can most effectively acquire a second language when the task of language learning becomes incidental to the task of communicating. Conversation in both formal and informal settings is part of the Socializing process through which children learn a "living language," which, like all living things, changes and adapts to the stimuli of its environment. Socializing fosters communication couched in language that is not artificially contrived, but that develops naturally as part of a reaching-out to meet and converse with other people.

A Yellow Ribbon

It is sharing time in the classroom. Miguel has brought in an Easter basket. Although Miguel is relatively inexperienced in communicating in English, he is anxious to share his basket with the class. Miguel communicates in English with Spanish intrusions; he relies on his Spanish to fill in for words that are not part of his limited English vocabulary. Miguel tells the class about his basket with little smiles and gestures; then the teacher encourages the class to raise hands and question him about his basket. Miguel calls on Adeleine. She asks, "What color is the ribbon?" Miguel repeats the word, "Ribbon?" He becomes very self-conscious and blushes. His lack of understanding of the word makes him unable to respond. His eyes search the classroom as if looking for a cue of some kind.

Miguel: This basket. I'm got little candy for . . . for . . . for día de Pascua (Easter). I'm got huevos de colores (colored eggs) blue, green, yellow. I'm got little pollitos (chicks). Me sit and eat chocolate con mi hermana (with my sister).

Teacher: Girls and boys, now you may ask Miguel questions about his basket. Remember to raise your hands!

Adeleine: (Raising hand.) What color is the ribbon?

Miguel: Ribbon? (Taken aback by the unfamiliar word "ribbon," looks around the classroom as if searching for a cue to the meaning. Finally, his gaze rests on María. María points to the ribbon in Adeleine's hair; Miguel has found his cue.)

Miguel: A yellow ribbon! (Looks to Adeleine for confirmation. Adeleine nods yes. Miguel is elated.)

Carlos: Can I have the green egg you have in your Easter basket?

Miguel: What? (Looks puzzled.)

Carlos: Can I have the green egg? Look—Look—Look—(forms an egg shape with his hands).

Miguel: (Stares in basket.)

Carlos: Green egg. (Gets up and points to the green egg in basket.)

Miguel: (Smiling.) O.K. Here green egg!

INFERENCING-GUESSING STRATEGY
AND SECOND-LANGUAGE LEARNING
CUE ME IN

"A yellow ribbon!"—"Here a green egg." Miguel says these phrases in the context of the communicative interaction, first with Adeleine and then with Carlos, and it is clear that he has derived meaning from the words. Miguel has decoded the English words he initially didn't understand and has communicated in the second language largely as the result of his successful use of cues for linguistic problem solving. He has made use of the **Cue Me In** strategy.

Miguel is typical of many children in the early acquisition stages of second language. He wants to express himself but is handicapped by his limited vocabulary and linguistic comprehension. Until he can speak fairly proficiently, he has to find ways to get by without much language. To get by in the sharing situation, where he is expected to give information and then respond to questions, Miguel must set about linguistic problem solving. Miguel's first dilemma is to find an easy way to structure sentences so he can tell the class about his basket. He resolves this expressive problem by allowing Spanish intrusions to penetrate his English discourse. When Miguel does not have the English word to express himself, he inserts its Spanish equivalent. Miguel comes upon the solution to his comprehension problem when María points to the ribbon and gives him a cue to the meaning of the word. Miguel finds that by becoming particularly alert to environmental cues he can gain an understanding of the second language. Miguel thus adopts the Cue Me In strategy. This strategy is characterized by its clue search and by its information extracting trait. It allows the second-language learner to make inferences or guesses about the meanings of words not yet fully understood. The cue is the hint or signal that makes inferencing possible. Cues provide the information needed to make sense out of individual words or phrases in a given communicative utterance and hence construct the bridge to total comprehension.

Cues are given to second-language learners by more proficient speakers or are derived by the learner himself from the nature of the verbal interaction. Cues can be visual, gestural involving sensory-motor actions, linguistic, and interpersonal. The Cue Me In strategy permits the second-language learner to do one or more of the following to decode a verbal message: pay attention to visual cues, such as concrete objects or pictures that represent the lexical item; interpret the speaker's gestures; try to discern the meaning from context; guess the gist of the conversation using linguistic cues; and remain alert to interpersonal feedback. The strategy stresses cued linguistic comprehension. Understanding leads to increased production and eventually to communicative competence (Hymes 1974). The effectiveness of the strategy depends on the learner's sensitivity to cues, as well as on his ability to form hypotheses.

Bialystok (1978) states, "Inferencing from cues may provide an effective means of improving linguistic production in formal or informal situations because it allows the learner to generate a reasonable hypothesis about something being expressed." The function of a cue, then, is to provide the stimulus for hypotheses formation which leads to the association of an unknown word with a known concept. In the second language, words standing alone have no inherent meaning. The words become meaningful only when they become attached to an existing schema or concept that the second-language learner possesses. Thus, the word "ribbon" became meaningful to Miguel when María's pointing cued him to the word's visual referent.

Visual cues are among the most productive cues because they give the second-language learner a great deal to go on in forming a hypothesis about the meaning of a word (MacNamara and Seymour 1971). Visual cues provide the learner with a concrete or pictorial representation of a word. Visual cues make it possible for an item to transit from an auditory to a visual state (Nelson 1977). The second-language learner who is sensitive to visual cues can immediately infer meaning by making a connection between what is seen and what is heard. Visual cues can be as effective at evoking comprehension of an unknown word as a direct translation of the word into the child's first language. Another advantage of visual cues is that they enable the child to decode words quickly enough so as not to interrupt the flow of communication, thus giving him or her confidence in communicating in the second language. Tovey (1976) believes that the ability to infer the meaning of words from visual cues is vital for the second-language learner. This fact is especially apparent in the situation Miguel was faced with as he attempted to share his Easter basket.

Miguel was struggling to communicate to his peers not only with his words, but with his feelings. Each time he realized he didn't know an appropriate English word he substituted the Spanish word to keep the flow of hs discourse going. Yet, when Adeleine asked him the question, "What color is the ribbon?" his feelings of inadequacy to understand the word "ribbon" caused him to become speechless. He wanted to respond but was left with the realization that he had not understood the question totally. In Miguel's case, the unfamiliarity with the word label was sufficient to indicate a failure to comprehend the question. He proceeded by engaging in a number of constructive processes which constitute the Cue Me In strategy. Bransford and Franks (1971) state that when comprehension does not occur, children engage in a variety of constructive processes, such as looking for cues which operate upon linguistic information to transform it into meaningful input. Miguel's first attempt at comprehension was to repeat the word "ribbon," hoping to get a linguistic cue from the word itself. To Miguel, the word seemed like a masked messenger of meaning. The word was masked because Miguel had no idea of its referent. Miguel then began to search for the referent. He toured the classroom with his eyes as if he had to probe his way carefully through a maze of visual stimuli until he found the cue he needed. María, sensitive to Miguel's seeking behavior, pointed to the ribbon in Adeleine's hair. María's cue provided Miguel with the concrete referent for the word. He immediately understood; the word was unmasked!

Weiner et al. (1972) state that verbal understandings often are helped by nonverbal, appropriate visual cues that serve to further explain meanings. Miguel's immediate understanding is partially the result of María's appropriate visual cue, but it is also due to the fact that Miguel had already formed the concept of a ribbon and knew the label in his first language. Miguel now has only to bridge the English label to the concept. Miguel's conceptual understanding enables him to attach the English word "ribbon" to its physical representation in Adeleine's hair. Shertzer (1968) defines understanding as the ability to infer meaning and significance from the sender's nonverbal message and then to use the meaning for effective communication. Miguel's comprehension leads to effective communication as he answers Adeleine's question emphatically, "A yellow ribbon!" His response clearly demonstrates that he has inferred meaning from María's nonverbal, visual cue.

Seeking visual cues is one of the most efficient strategies utilized by second-language learners. Corder (1966) notes that:

> Whereas in content-subjects knowledge of the subject is attained through a combination of linguistic and sensory experience, in second-language learning it is precisely the language which is the object of learning, with sensory experience and knowledge of the world being the means. Visual aids of all kinds thus take on a reality which is unique; they take on the burden of meaning which in content-subjects is shared with language.

Visual cues that are closely associated with language may be said to facilitate the initial acquisition of language. Bilinguals develop a sensitivity to visual cues. Ben-Zeev (1975) gives evidence that relying on visual cues as a strategy is often well developed in bilinguals. In a Spanish-English study which included several different methods to test sensitivity to visual cues, bilinguals were noted to score higher on the WISC Picture Completion subtest which measures perception of visual details. The author explains the bilinguals' high scores on this subtest by relating it to the natural visual scanning bilinguals engage in when learning a second language. Sensitivity to visual details is presumed to be developed as bilinguals search for visual cues as a means to establish meaning for unknown words.

Piaget (1952) points out the primacy of encoding by children. When children are acquiring a first language they usually learn words only after they have experienced the visual or physical representation of the words. Children play with a train or see a train and learn to associate the word "train" with the object. Words often are tied intrinsically to actions. DeLaguna (1963) comments that "to understand what the child is saying you must see what he is doing." Second-language learners also rely on sensory input and action sequences to make an association of an English word to a known object or event. In fact, usually the more visual input the second-language learner receives the more he or she is able to abstract meaning from linguistic utterances. The more information received behind the eyeball, the less linguistic information need be processed.

Another type of cue used by the second-language learner is a gestural or sensory-motor cue. Love and Roderick (1971) define gestural cues as "that aspect of body motion that evokes meaning within contextual situations." Gestures serve to clarify, elaborate, direct or guide the second-language learner in understanding the verbal message. Research done by Swenson (1975) on cues utilized by beginning language learners manifested that pointing to an object is a gesture that can be considered one of the most salient sensory-motor cues because it guides the learner's directional focus and therefore expedites comprehension. María's pointing behavior cued Miguel where to concentrate his attention to attain meaning. Werner (1948) has described the gesture of pointing as one of the most primitive ways of communicating through the use of sensory-motor cues. Carlos communicates to Miguel that he wants "a green egg" by pointing to the green egg in Miguel's basket. Miguel does not understand the words "a green egg," but as Carlos says the words accompanied by the pointing gesture he is able to bridge the meaning to the words. Bruner and Kenney (1965) and Gagné (1974) regard pointing activity as a means of getting the learner's attention to critical visual cues that will aid him in decoding meaning. Pointing is an enforced-attention procedure. Lee and Dobson (1977) state that visual cues combined with pointing activity are two important variables in second-language learning. The pointing gesture serves to direct the learner's attention to a visual image. Lee and Dobson believe that the second-language learner should use the cueing strategy of pointing when learning a word in the new language. They encourage that the child not only look at an object or picture and say the word, but point to the object also. In a study of eighty-four children in elementary school, Lee and Dobson found that those children who were taught words using visual and gestural cues learned words more easily than either of the groups who used visual or verbal cues alone. Daehler et al. (1969) found verbal rehearsal, when combined with pointing to color representations, facilitated the recall of the names of colors by children. It can be inferred from the cited research that the more modalities a second-language learner can exercise in learning a word, the more easily the student will master it and the better he or she will retain it. The total number of modalities has an additive and positive effect on language learning.

Carter (1974) did an analysis of communicative development. She found a series of gestural schemata which could be differentiated with high probability. Pointing to objects was one of the most prominent gestures that occurred as children learned the names for objects. MacNamara and Baker (1975) discovered that children learning a second language initially were heavily influenced by gestures and often pointed to objects as they named them. The authors found that as the children mastered the language, gestures were used less frequently.

Gestures in the form of pantomime cue the second-language learner to the meaning of words and phrases. Carlos, before pointing to the egg in Miguel's basket, forms an egg with his hand to help Miguel interpret the meaning of the word "egg." Bloomfield (1933) described various gestures which cue children in the earliest stages of language learning to the meaning of words.

> Pointing to the object is one kind of gestural cue; sitting down and standing up is another; using the hands to define a circular shape is a third; a fourth is lifting an imaginary cup to one's lips to evoke, "I drink."

These gestural cues serve the function of directing attention to a specific object, depicting properties of the object, and pantomiming actions that match words. There also are certain codified gestures that imply meaning, such as hand, palm up, means stop (Stewig 1979). All these gestural cues permit the second-language learner to translate the meaning of verbal communication.

Understanding cues is largely dependent upon the context of the utterance, the situation, topic, and setting. Bloom (1970) has shown that identification of meaning is dependent on relating the linguistic utterance to the contextual features. Cues depend on context to the extent that they clarify or define the situation in which the verbal interaction is occurring (French 1975). Miguel understood María's gestural cue of pointing to the ribbon because it related directly to Adeleine's preceding question, "What color is the ribbon?" Were Miguel engaged in playing with a train, pointing to the ribbon would serve no communicative purpose because it would not fit the context.

Whitehurst (1977) suggests that young children can communicate successfully by the efficient utilization of context cues. Four studies on cued recall done by Barclay et al. (1974) found cues to be most effective when they were related to events described previously. Tulving and Thomson (1973) report that for a cue to be effective it must be suitably related to the context. The authors suggest that children can learn word meanings through cues that are directly related to the word's semantic properties or to the representation of the word. Strom and Ray (1975) did a number of toy-talk experiments. In these experiments, children might be shown a group of soldiers and then given the word "fewer" along with the gesture of removing some of the soldiers. Children learned the word "fewer" through the physical representation of its meaning in context.

Ervin-Tripp (1977) speaks of context cues as "situational meaning." She says situational meaning is essential for the interpretation of speech as it shapes the perceptual surface of speech and so shapes the cognitive frame by highlighting certain possible interpretations rather than others. A pointing gesture over one's shoulder could take on different meanings in differing contexts. Gestures must be intimately related to the verbal context to guide second-language learners in their quest for meaning. Fillmore (1976) speaks of the way English speakers fitted their cues to a given situation to enable Spanish speakers to comprehend the language.

> They generally created contexts to make what they were saying clear and interpretable. They did this by means of gestures, demonstrations, and clarifications. Speech was limited to what they were doing. The speech either accompanied an action or predicted one.

The second-language learners thus came to rely on context cues as a strategy to increased understanding of the situation in which they found themselves. Fillmore further describes the process that second-language learners followed to derive cues from context in the following maxim: "Assume what people are saying is directly relevant to the situation at hand, or what they or you are experiencing."

Rubin (1975) describes the good language learner as a good guesser. Guessing and inference-making are the essential processes that result from the Cue Me In strategy. Second-language learners using this strategy rely on a variety of cues to narrow down the meaning of a communicative intent. Miguel, in another conversation with María, did not understand her when she used the word "smaller." María cued him by stooping down to show she was smaller. It may be noted that the Cue Me In strategy can take on game-like qualities, and therefore has special appeal for children.

Willingness to hypothesize about meaning, to guess the meaning of an unknown word, is a crucial skill in second-language learning (Grittner 1980). Learning a new language provides an enormous amount of practice in this skill. Such a skill involves, furthermore, many important related skills, such as using all available information, tolerating ambiguity and judging when to remain tentative and when to assign definite meaning to a new word. The cue is any communicative instance that stimulates the learner to make an inference. Even though second-language learners may be exposed to cues that clarify the meaning of a word, Carton (1966) notes that individuals vary according to their propensity for making inference, tolerance of risk, and ability to make valid, rational, and reasonable inferences. Carton suggests four steps which are involved in inference-making or guessing:

1. scanning the environment for a cue
2. making a hypothesis
3. assessment of probability that inference is correct
4. readjustment to later information

Miguel applied Carton's four steps to make an inference about the meaning of the word "ribbon." 1) He visually scanned the environment searching for a cue and became aware of María's pointing gesture. 2) He formed a hypothesis that the object María was pointing to was the physical representation of the word "ribbon." 3) He assessed the probability he was correct by watching Adeleine's face as he said the words, "A yellow ribbon!" 4) Adeleine's nod told him he had decoded the cue and answered her question correctly. If Adeleine had not given him confirmatory feedback, Miguel would have had to reassess his interpretation of the cue to make another response. A good part of learning a language involves this kind of feedback. The learner must make guesses in trying out newly acquired language forms. Cues guide the second-language learner to make more right than wrong guesses. Often the provision of a cue aids the learner also in selecting among alternatives (Dillon and Bittner 1975). Miguel knows Carlos wants something from his Easter basket. Carlos' gestural cue of forming an egg with his hands helps Miguel to choose the egg over the other items in his basket. The fact that Miguel chooses correctly indicates that Carlos has given him an effective cue. Tulving and Donaldson (1972) say hypothesis forming is directly related to cue effectiveness. Cue effectiveness in turn depends on the strength of the association of the cue with the word.

In addition to visual, gestural, and contextual cues, the second-language learner depends on linguistic cues to ascertain meaning in three ways. First, he abstracts meaning by using what he knows about the rules of speaking (Paulston 1974). Secondly, he attends to content words as indicators of communicative intent (Mueller and Baker 1972). Finally, he relies on the sensitivity of peers to cue him in to meaning by simplifying and clarifying verbal input.

Children's sensitivity to the needs of beginning language learners has been demonstrated in various studies. Shatz and Gelman (1973) gave evidence that four-year-olds modified and simplified their speech considerably when talking to still younger children. It has been noted that English-speaking children in a bilingual class cue Spanish speakers linguistically by simplifying and clarifying their utterances. Berko-Gleason (1973) illustrated also that children adjust their speech level for the sake of second-language learners. The ability to do so is a pragmatic skill. Children at a fairly young age are aware of the special needs of language learners. They are adept at taking the perspective of the learner and are responsive to their capacity to respond and comprehend. The nature of adjustments made by children indicates they have some intuition of linguistic complexity. This is especially exemplified by the way children emphasize content words which carry the meaning of communication. They simplify and clarify their sentences to emphasize the most meaningful linguistic elements. Carlos cued Miguel linguistically first by simplifying his question, "Can I have the green egg you have in your Easter basket?" to "Can I have the green egg?" to finally "green egg" accompanied by a pointing gesture. Carlos was aware of Miguel's failure to comprehend his first question, so he simplified his question linguistically and then clarified the meaning by using the gestural cue of pointing. Carlos' sensitive cueing adapted to Miguel's ability to comprehend.

Another form of linguistic cues are words used as attention-getters. Words serve as attention-getters when they signal attention to a specific cue to meaning about to be given. Carlos said to Miguel, "Look—Look—Look" before he produced the gestural cue of forming his hands in the shape of an egg. Fillmore (1976) observed that the less proficient a child was in the second language the more English-speaking peers used the attention-getters for cueing, such as: "Look, Watch, and See," rather than attention-holding expressions as "Hey and OK." Fillmore described linguistic cueing in the classroom she studied:

> They seemed to signal or alert the second-language learner that the utterances which followed were intended for his or her ears. There were expressions that were frequently repeated, such as "Look at and Watch this." Structures tended to clarify verbal input as well with statements such as, "See I'm making a round thing."

The linguistic cues that children supply second-language learners make it possible for them to construe meaning from verbal utterances more easily.

In addition to the linguistic cues of simplification, clarification, and attentional markers, second-language learners become acutely aware of phonological cues. Because of their limited comprehension of the second language, children are supersensitive to the tone of a message or to the manner in which something is said. Tone and stress given to individual words or phrases cue learners to the intent of the message. Ervin-Tripp (1973) refers to tone and stress cues as making the contrast between asking, demanding, and commenting. Miguel was aware that Adeleine was asking him a question because of the intonational patterns he has come to understand that are part of question-asking. Second-language learners develop a feeling for those phonological cues which best enhance intelligibility (Rubin 1975). They may look for intonation patterns over individual sounds because of the close relationship of these patterns with meaning.

Finally, second-language learners pay close attention to interpersonal cues. They use peer feedback in the strategy of Cue Me In. The learners produce an utterance and then await acceptance or verification of their linguistic expression by confirmatory feedback from peers. This feedback is often kinetic, such as a smile, frown or a look of bewilderment. Adeleine's nod was the interpersonal cue Miguel needed to determine that he had communicated adequately. There is a good deal of evidence to suggest that normal human interaction depends to some extent on nonverbal interpersonal cues which permit dialogue to take place within a given framework. It is important to note that smiling, nodding, and maintaining eye contact not only cues in the other dialogue-partner but also encourages him or her to continue the conversation (Ward et al. 1974; Rosenfeld 1966). Facial expressions, especially, are effective interpersonal cues (Love and Roderick 1971). Eye communication has long been accorded special consideration because of the general belief that eyes are the "gateway to the mind." Eye communication gives second-language learners an indication of the amount of comprehension taking place.

According to a study conducted by Rosenthal and Jacobson (1968) reported in their book *Pygmalion in the Classroom*, nonverbal interpersonal cues may play a significant role in the development of meaning. The amount of meaning derived from interpersonal cues is related directly to the amount of feedback a person receives and the receptivity and sensitivity to that feedback. The second-language learner is receptive to feedback cues not only to ascertain the extent of comprehension of the dialogue-partner, but also to change and modify utterances according to the feedback. The cooperation, then, of peers who speak the second language more fluently is important to children who are trying to perfect their communication skills. Familiarity may encourage the cooperation and interaction between learners and more proficient speakers of the target language.

Interpersonal cueing is also a means of emotional reinforcement for the student. Emotional forces may foster sensitivity to interpersonal cues (Hornby 1977). The child is likely to make mistakes by interpreting stimuli from one language as belonging to the other. The degree of acceptance he or she finds for his or her mistakes is manifested by the interpersonal cues. Positive interpersonal feedback by the more proficient speaker aids the learner as an attempt is made to express himself or herself.

In summary, the Cue Me In strategy is used by second-language learners to derive meaning from verbal input. This strategy is dependent on the types of hints, clues, signals or suggestions given by peers, teachers, or the speech setting. There are several types of cues to which students become sensitive as they endeavor to understand and communicate in the second language. Visual cues alert learners to a word's referent. Gestural cues direct learners' attention to environmental features or clarify an utterance through sensory-motor actions. Contextual cues refer learners back to the situation or setting of the speech act. Linguistic cues serve to simplify or clarify verbal utterances, or function as attentional markers. Phonological cues, such as tone or stress, suggest the intent of the message. Finally, interpersonal cues give children the feedback they need to interpret how effectively their verbal expression is being received. Students learning a second language apply these cues as a strategy to infer or guess the meaning of linguistic input. Children rely on more proficient language speakers to give them cues because they are aided by greater vocabulary and more shared word associations (Palermo 1963). The second-language learner, because of his or her strong desire to communicate, actively seeks to interpret cues which will help decode the meaning of language and allow participation to the fullest extent possible in what Hymes (1972) terms the "speech community."

IMPLICATIONS OF CUE ME IN FOR SECOND-LANGUAGE LEARNING AND CLASSROOM TEACHING

Cues are the "keys" students naturally use to unlock the meanings of words in the second language and enter into communication in that language. It is incumbent upon teachers to build on the strategy of Cue Me In when teaching the second language and encouraging social interaction. The teaching-learning process should be considered within a communications framework. From this perspective, both teachers and students serve as senders and receivers of verbal messages as well as nonverbal signals and cues. French (1970) reports significant findings on the nature of classroom activities classified as "communication events." These events are characterized by the active participation of teacher and students in meaningful social discourse. Cues enhance the understanding of second-language learners when the cues fit into the communicative flow. Hart (1975) suggests that communication is limited in classrooms where cueing procedures are not employed to elicit production. All types of cueing should be highlighted in the classroom. Cues serve as hints to meaning. Students depend greatly on the Cue Me In strategy to decode verbal input. Many classroom teachers tend to discourage this natural communication strategy by admonishing students not to guess. Twaddell (1973) recognizes the importance of guessing and inferencing for second-language learning. Twaddell makes the following suggestions to teachers:

1. Encourage students to transfer what they know about the world to the new language.
2. Teach vocabulary related to concepts children are familiar with.
3. Have students practice attending to the formal features of language.
4. Help students accept temporary vagueness in the early stages of learning.

These suggestions make learning a second language more in accord with the natural communication process where the participants in discourse do not always hear, understand or interpret what is being said to them; still they do not panic but continue the conversation to see whether the unclear verbal input will be clarified in the course of dialogue. The key here is learning through active participation.

The active participation method of teaching a second language is in direct contrast to the passive repetition method. It is active in the sense that children are encouraged to make guesses or inferences in order that they may participate to a greater degree in communicative exchanges with more proficient speakers. Emphasis is on inferring meaning and continuing the flow of discourse, rather than on grammatical perfection of form sentences. Cueing is a significant part of the active participation method.

Visual cueing is practiced by teachers to enable students to make a connection of words with the things they represent. Rohwer et al. (1967) reported that children learned paired words when they were presented with pictures. This particular study states, "It seems that an informed and selective use of pictorial representations and verbal labels and contexts will result in more efficient learning of language." Asher and Parke (1975) describe a word pairing game that facilitates second-language learning. In the game, students are taught a number of things that relate to each other. Picture cues are used. The children form teams; each team has the other's associated items. Children must verbally request the picture that goes with the picture they hold, thus making an associated pair. The game can be extended by having children use magazines to find pictures of things that go together. These pictures can be placed on cards and used for the "Go Fish" game. The student asks a team member, "Do you have something that goes with a baseball?" The teacher can encourage further language usage by asking children to explain why the items go together.

Another game that teaches language through use of cueing was designed by Gordon and Flavell (1974). The game proceeds as follows:

> The teacher brings to class a closed box full of familiar objects such as nails, balls, soap, food, etc. (Objects can be integrated with the current theme of study.) Students take turns coming to get an object from the box. Objects should be of the instructor's choice so as to ensure the unknown identity of the remaining content of the box. A student who has just been given an object stays at the back of the classroom, so that the rest of the class will not see the object, and begins to describe it in English. When the object has been identified, the student shows the object to the class and the teacher writes the name of the object on the board.

This game requires the second-language learner to communicate with the expressions he or she knows to describe the object.

Writing words and drawing pictures to represent verbal labels are effective methods for vocabulary learning. Concentrating on word labels that match pictures enables second-language learners to actively build a working vocabulary. The game of "What's Missing?" builds upon visual cues in the form of pictures that children remember in association with their word labels. The game is played by:

> . . . presenting four pictures to children. Children are taught the label for each picture. The teacher then lines up the pictures and asks the children to close their eyes. The teacher removes one picture. The children must recall the label for the picture which has been removed.

This game is effective for vocabulary building because it encourages concentration on and retention of the word labels. Games with visual representation provide a learning sequence that moves from visual to verbal. This sequence acts spontaneously to offer cues for language development.

Pictures by themselves can act as stimuli for language production. Manzo and Legenza (1975) attempted to predict the types of pictures that activate language usage. He used the Picture Potency Formula and found that the more of each of the following characteristics that was contained in the picture the more language stimulation was provoked. The characteristics include:

1. different things in picture
2. different colors
3. children present
4. actions in progress
5. people present
6. things with potential movement

   Other important factors are:

7. compatibility with interests and experiences of the children with whom it is to be used
8. racial similarities
9. empathetic qualities of setting (urban, rural)
10. familiarity with event being depicted
11. size of picture (larger pictures are better)

Pictures can function as language stimulants. Discussing individual items in the picture builds vocabulary; describing actions furthers expressive ability. Learners can describe a wide variety of things in a picture. Some children, however, may need to be cued by the teacher to look at certain aspects of the picture to reduce information to a manageable level. For example, pointing to a rabbit's mouth limits attention to the carrot; chomping movements of the teacher's jaws may direct learners toward verbs for eating, biting, chewing, etc.; raised eyebrows and an intent gaze as well as linguistic intonation can suggest questions about the rabbit's behavior. The teacher's nonverbal cues may not actually produce the correct reply, but will reduce the range of potentially acceptable replies and thus simplify and clarify verbal input.

Visual cues to teach vocabulary are most effective when combined with contextual cues. The practice of teaching words in a context of relevant materials is what British linguists call "collocations." With this method, students learn words that are associated with a theme or topic. Context also may be used to teach connective and relational words. The context itself cues children to word meaning. A theme of "Under the Sea" would cue learners to the meaning of the word "under" as he or she ties it to the context of the study. Physical demonstration in the context of instruction also cues meaning. For example, if the instruction were, "Put the red bead in the cup," the teacher could point to the red bead (gestural cue) as she said the words "red bead," and actually put the bead in the cup. This technique produces the assimilation of the concrete perceptual information simultaneously with the language. Corsini (1969), in an experiment on language learning, discovered that when nonverbal cues were presented simultaneously with a verbal instruction, retention was significantly greater than with verbal instruction alone. This is consistent with the importance Montessori (1965) placed on sensory-motor actions. Montessori wrote that children learning a language need sensory-motor input to derive meaning. Acting out what words specify makes language more personal and understandable to the second-language learner.

Teachers making use of linguistic cueing can capitalize on the fact that children are helped to predict or infer what they haven't mastered in oral language. Verbal expression which is used daily with only minor variations becomes highly predictable and is easily reproduced. Children can discern the meanings of utterances by observing how they relate to the activities going on in the classroom and noticing what their classmates do in response. In this way, context cues enable them to function as though understanding what is going on long before they understand the language. Teachers can encourage children's use of context cues by employing the same expressions with gestures for daily procedural commands. Consistency in this regard is most important. Pointing to the door each day before recess and saying the words, "It's time to line up," gives a learner the cue to decode the command. Such cues given throughout the day are most helpful to the student.

Two major functions of the teacher's cueing are to demonstrate meaning and promote dialogue. Grant and Henning (1971) point out that in many classroom interactions there is little face-to-face dialogue. Utterances by themselves are akin to the telephone conversation in which the absence of visual cues makes comprehension more difficult. Gestures, body movement, and facial expressions convey meaning and promote understanding.

Cueing the second-language learner in the classroom situation has far-reaching advantages. It does the following:

1. prompts students to infer meaning and answer correctly

2. encourages active participation over passive repetition

3. gives corrective feedback

4. directs the learner's attention

5. makes explicit what normally goes unmarked

Teachers can implement the strategy of Cue Me In as a technique to support inference-making by second-language learners. The teacher can be thought of as a stage director who, with skill and sensitivity, gives the appropriate cues that encourage the fluent flow of the dialogue.

Say It Again

It is lunch recess at the school. Miguel is waiting impatiently on the ice cream line with the other children. Becoming bored with the wait, he turns around and chats in Spanish with María. Unknowingly, he reaches the front of the line and is startled by the lady selling ice cream as she inquires, "What kind do you want?" It is obvious that Miguel has understood her because he replies, "helado de chocolate." The lady responds with "What?" Miguel turns red. He snatches his money off the counter and runs away from the ice cream line to a bench in the school yard, where he sits in a dejected manner. Meanwhile, María, next in turn on the ice cream line, asks for and gets chocolate ice cream. She then joins Miguel on the bench.

María: ¿Por qué no le pediste helado a la señora?
         (Why didn't you ask the lady for ice cream?)

Miguel: No puedo decirlo en inglés.
         (I can't say it in English.)

María: Claro que puedes decirlo—helado de chocolate—chocolate ice cream.
         (Sure, you can say it—chocolate ice cream.)

Miguel: Dímelo otra vez.
         (Say it again.)

María: Chocolate ice cream.

Miguel: Choc lat ice —
         Dímelo otra vez. (Say it again.)

María: Chocolate ice cream.

Miguel: Chocolate ice creama.
         Dímelo otra vez. (Say it again.)

María: Chocolate ice cream.

Miguel: Chocolate ice cream.

María: Sí.

(Miguel gets back in line and asks for, and gets, chocolate ice cream.)

IMITATIVE-REPETITIVE STRATEGY AND SECOND-LANGUAGE LEARNING
PEER PROMPTING

"Dímelo otra vez." Miguel asks María to tell him again and again the words, "chocolate ice cream." He imitates and repeats the words until he can say them correctly. In this example, Miguel has employed the strategy of **Peer Prompting** to learn the vocabulary of the second language. María's prompting enables Miguel to learn the English words he needs to express a desire. María prompts Miguel by repeating the words several times so Miguel can imitate them. The success of the strategy is apparent since Miguel is able to ask for and receive a chocolate ice cream.

Children often experience enormous difficulty in getting their message across when speaking in a second language, and many of them come to rely on their peers as language models. Fillmore (1976), in her study of Spanish-speaking children learning English, found that one of the strategies leading to fluency in English was "Count on your friends for help." Fillmore observed that children encouraged each other to learn new words by repeating them slowly in order to facilitate the peer's imitation. Children learned to communicate in the second language by imitating peers and bringing these imitations into closer approximation of the peer's utterance. Montessori (1912) notes that children learning a language are badly in need of a model who will enunciate and repeat words for them to imitate. María was Miguel's language model. She said the words "chocolate ice cream" slowly and distinctly. Miguel imitated the words several times, getting closer and closer to the exact pronunciation. María finally confirmed his exact imitation as she said, "Sí."

Imitation is an important part of the strategy of Peer Prompting. Imitation is defined by Ramer (1976) as those utterances which the child produces that repeat exactly all or part of an immediately preceding utterance of another speaker. The child's production does not add to nor change the model's utterance. Thus, Miguel's reponse to María's prompting can be classified as imitation because he repeated exactly what María said. Ramer also mentions that in order for imitation to occur at all, there must be some previously established knowledge of the concept underlying the word(s). Miguel's concept of chocolate ice cream was very real, and he knew its label in his first language. Miguel was imitating the English words to give the object its linguistic label in English. Imitation is a means for learning and practicing the linguistic labels for known concepts. Nelson (1973) found imitation occurred with high frequency whenever there was meaning attached to words. Piaget (1969) asserted that verbal imitiation without meaning tends to be immediately forgotten. True verbal learning is learning not only by imitating, but also by understanding.

Bloom et al. (1974) observed the function of imitation in early language and found that children utilized imitation to give words to the concepts they had already experienced actively. Hammerly (1971) states that words are learned by directly relating them to ongoing experiences. For example, Miguel and María may be playing with a ball when María introduces the English word "ball" to Miguel. Miguel knows what a ball is and can easily tie the English word to the object. Montessori (1912), in her discussion on language learning, makes it clear that the child will imitate a peer's or teacher's word for an object only after he has conceived the idea of the object represented by the word. Nelson (1973) asserts that children use imitation at certain points in the language acquisition process. Children's imitations are functionally characterized by the existence of the concept prior to the imitated expression of words. Concepts precede verbal imitation in the strategy of Peer Prompting, also. Before children solicit the words from a peer for an object or concept, the meanings of the prompted words are already understood. Children adopt this strategy when they want to communicate a message in a second language but lack the words to express it. Therefore, their intent is to have their peers prompt them by modeling the English words that fit the situation or social interaction.

A knowledge of intent is important in the process of imitation exercised in the strategy. Intent gives added meaning to the imitative process. Children imitate words with an intent. The intent may be to communicate, to interact with others, to solve a problem, or to satisfy a need. Children imitate the words that match their intent. Ervin-Tripp (1977) states that one of the characteristics of imitation is that it can be described by alluding to the child's intent, as a request for information, request for services, or an assertion. Imitation that is practiced in the Peer Prompting strategy relies on situational intent and on the shared knowledge of intent. This shared knowledge of intent allows the peer to prompt the learner by selectively verbalizing the words the learner requires to satisfy his desires or to interact socially. Miguel's intent was to make a request for ice cream in English. María, as a member of the same speech community as Miguel, was able to communicate with him in Spanish to discover his intent. María's knowledge of Miguel's desire allowed her to structure the verbal interaction by prompting Miguel with the English words he needed. It is clear that María's prompting was effective as Miguel's smile shows satisfaction in the ice cream and in his successful communication with the ice cream vendor.

Hoffman (1934) suggests that prompting is one of the most effective ways to learn second-language vocabulary because it not only gives the learner feedback on the correct words needed in a given situation, but it also provides the opportunity for the learner to imitate and repeat. Ervin-Tripp (1964) notes that an outstanding characteristic of peer imitative interactions is their sheer repetitiveness.

Repetition and imitation are indeed related in the strategy of Peer Prompting. Repetition is the means by which children practice the words they first imitate. It is defined by Nelson (1973) as the immediate sequence of the same or highly similar form of verbal production. Repetition, like imitation, is appropriate at a point where language acquisition has begun but has not yet advanced. It is a functional part of language learning and builds on the process of imitation by making it possible for the learner to practice the language forms that he or she needs to communicate. It is seen as a two-way process in Peer Prompting. The peer model uses repetition to encourage the learner to imitate the language forms correctly. The language-learner peer uses insistent repetition to phonetically reproduce an utterance that matches that of the peer model. Repetition can be recognized as a two-way process in the dialogue of Miguel and María. Miguel's repetition (of the words "chocolate ice cream") was sustained by María's repetitive feedback.

Whitehurst (1976) did a study to examine the effects on the development of communication by the repetitive feedback given by the models. He noted that repetitive peer feedback made it possible for language learners to become increasingly able to meet the requirements of informative communication. Good modeling was described as informative, meaningful, repetitive verbal behavior. María's prompting of Miguel included both repetitive feedback and meaningful communication, which Whitehurst describes as elements of good modeling. María's feedback made it possible for Miguel not only to copy her words, but to successfully communicate in the second language.

One of the classic findings in the literature of human learning and memory is that repetition facilitates learning (Ebbinghaus 1885). Much later, Peterson et al. (1977) found repetition facilitated the retention of verbal information when words were connected to meaningful messages. Shiffrin and Atkinson (1969) also found that repetition was beneficial and had an excellent effect on students' learning language tasks, especially when the tasks required semantic over phonetic processing; thus confirming that learners remembered words they repeated when there was meaning attached to the words, and failed to learn words that were connected only by having similar sounds. Although Miguel sounded out the words "chocolate ice cream" to imitate María, he not only learned a series of sounds, he also had an attached meaning to the words.

Miguel's emerging ability to use the second language can be expressed as cognitive growth. One of the features of cognitive growth which Piaget and Montessori observed, and to which they both attached considerable importance, is the frequently repetitive character of behaviors associated with mental capabilities that are beginning to appear (Elkind 1967). What Piaget and Montessori both recognized is the great role repetitive behavior plays in mental growth. Montessori (1912) observed that the child repeats over and over again words he or she has just learned. She termed this "polarization of attention." Montessori described repetitive behavior as the benchmark of maturing mental abilities.

Repetition is utilized in second-language learning to practice emerging expressive abilities. Piaget has pointed to the adaptive significance of the practice involved in children's repetitive behaviors. Piaget stated that children repeat to exercise their intellectual abilities. Piaget and Montessori alluded to repetitive behaviors as having tremendous value for the child's realization of a cognitive skill. Repetitive language behavior thus has value for the child learning a second language because it allows the child to practice the skill of expressing himself or herself in that language. Repetition and imitation eventually lead to spontaneous production.

In fact, a study by Ramer (1976) reported that imitative and repetitive usage of language led to later spontaneous production. This was understood to indicate that those forms which were initially imitated later became productive speech. It was assumed that this occurred because imitative utterances were transferred to social contexts. Miguel's imitative, repetitive practice of the words "chocolate ice cream" led to productive usage as he transferred the words from the practice situation with María to the actual communication with the ice cream vendor.

In summing up, then, repetition and imitation have been manifested as two essential and related components of the Peer Prompting strategy used naturally by children to learn a second language. Imitation permits the learner to copy the utterance of a peer model. Repetition builds practice into the strategy. It also provides the child with a communication check. As the second-language learner repeats words, the peer model repeats the words back to the learner. Repetition is then a dual process. The peer model prompts the learner by repeating words; the learner repeats to practice the words and to gain feedback from the model on his expressive accuracy.

Another essential element of the strategy is the meaning which the learner links to the second-language vocabulary. The strategy is not used as a means for learning concepts, but as a way of giving word labels to that which already has been learned cognitively and linguistically in the first language. Peer Prompting is always a part of an interaction in which the second-language learner seeks to express himself; and the peer model, recognizing this intent and the linguistic demands of the situation, prompts him appropriately. The second-language learner can take advantage of this strategy in many interchanges where he finds himself at a loss for the English words to express a communicative intent. The learner relies on peers to help master the vocabulary of the new communication system which he or she can then transfer meaningfully to other social contexts.

IMPLICATIONS OF <u>PEER PROMPTING</u> FOR SECOND-LANGUAGE LEARNING AND CLASSROOM TEACHING

The fact that children do learn from each other has long been acknowledged. Piaget (1965) has written on the stimulating effects of peer interaction on cognitive development. Piaget believes that schools should encourage and foster learning in which children can freely exchange ideas on common intellectual tasks close to their own interests. He states that these social interactions between peers have a powerful influence on cognitive development and may have a more powerful effect than adult-child exchanges (Piaget 1960, 1962, 1965, 1968). While Piaget does not refer specifically to second-language acquisition, the fact that learning a language is a cognitive task has educational implications for using peer interactions to foster second-language abilities. Children learn language from encounters with their environment that call for verbal exchanges. Peer transactions can act as stimuli to the development of linguistic fluency as children engage in tasks where language plays a dominant role. Language activities in the classroom can be well-framed to elicit language usage.

Peer dyads is one way of grouping children to promote language growth. A social studies curriculum, "Man: A Course of Study," developed by Bruner and others, places deliberate emphasis on peer dyads for many of the activities in order to encourage verbal problem solving (Hanley et al 1970). Dewey's (1902) writings also emphasized the cognitive growth which results from peer interaction. Dewey wrote that the school should organize itself on a social basis where friendship pairs of children teach each other in the spirit of social cooperation. Steinberg and Cazden (1979) focus on "instructional chains" as a method for children to learn a task from the teacher, and then, in turn, teach the task to other peers. They make it clear that the emphasis in this type of learning should be on the process. The process is one where verbal communication plays a dominant role. Speech is important to the context of peer learning activities for making requests, assertions, and giving directions. Thus, language is the medium for learners to communicate the essential details of any task. Since language is important to learning tasks, and children learn from each other, it is logical to pair learners with more proficient English speakers to encourage the learning of new language forms that are meaningful in that they are task-specific.

This concept of pairing students for language learning has been alluded to in the literature of the field. Finocchiaro (1958) talks about peer-pairs in second-language learning by stating: "It is only by relating to each other in experiences that language becomes meaningful. . . . Paired activities build opportunities for children to express themselves coupled with the goal of making friends." Thus, second-language learners paired with peers who are proficient English speakers not only acquire increased expressive ability, but also form new friendships. Nelson (1973) found exposure to language models had a facilitative effect on learning, particularly in vocabulary acquisition. Children who interacted the most frequently with models were judged to be more linguistically competent.

Seliger (1977) defines linguistic competence as the general ability to understand and make oneself understood. Seliger asserts that practice leads to linguistic competence. Practice is defined here as verbal interaction between two peers where one serves as the model. Children learning a second language seem to grasp automatically, through peer interactions, the linguistic structure and vocabulary. Second-language learners practice the new communication system by interacting intensively with English speakers around them.

The classroom teacher can extend interactions of second-language learners with more proficient English speakers through peer-pairing. Peer-pairs would consist of a dominant or proficient English speaker and a child who has limited expressive ability in the language. Children would be grouped in this manner for play interactions, as well as for specific subject-matter related activities. Each of the five Spanish-speaking children studied by Fillmore (1976) was, in fact, paired in this manner. Fillmore implemented the technique because she believed children learn language naturally from peer models. Children do learn language in this way, as evidenced by the strategy of Peer Prompting which they naturally adopt to acquire knowledge of a second language. An example of Peer Prompting that can occur in a classroom structured activity is explained in another interaction of Miguel and María—in a bingo game that was designed to teach classification. Miguel, who did not know the English name for some of the pictures, was prompted by María with the appropriate label. Miguel imitated the words and practiced them throughout the game. María's prompting gave Miguel the vocabulary necessary to participate in the game. The vocabulary learned by Miguel was intrinsically related to the game and served the goal of allowing him to interact with the other children.

MacNamara (1973) speaks of children paired for activities where conversation serves a practical goal. Peer models can help the inexperienced second-language learner master correct grammatical usage by expanding and thereby correcting the learner's speech in a meaningful social interaction. Thus, if the learner says, "He no is old," the model can naturally respond with, "My brother is not old either." In this way, the model unconsciously corrects and expands the learner's statement as a natural part of the ongoing dialogue. Witbeck (1976) writes about this type of peer modeling of linguistic structures which stresses back-and-forth communication among students. Maize (1952) found the advantage in peer correction of linguistic structures through natural dialogues was that it gave children extensive exposure to language forms in meaningful social exchanges.

Peer-pairing can thus serve as a method whereby children can acquire the vocabulary and linguistic structures of a second language through the prompting given by a peer who speaks the language well. Classroom teachers can maximize the effectiveness of this method by pairing students for a series of dyadic encounters in play situations. John and Carlos can be paired to play with the trucks. María and Cindy can be designated as buddies for lunch recess. In another technique, the teacher can devise language learning experiences through which the peer can model correct English grammar forms and vocabulary for the learner. For example, children can be paired to read a book together. The peer model gives word labels to pictures in the book, thus teaching vocabulary to the learner. Games that require verbal input also can serve as mediums for peer language modeling. Peer-paired math activities can be organized at any level of complexity. Math activities often require much verbal input as two children work together at problem solving.

The technique of peer-pairing is sufficiently flexible to be applied in an infinite number of ways throughout the school day, using subject-matter activities as well as play encounters. The most important factor relative to implementing peer-pairing is the interaction of two children getting together and becoming involved with language on an academic, personal, and emotional level.

Another method of pairing which can be termed "parrot pairs" denotes a two-person repetition game. Puppets are used in this type of game where children learn meaningful dialogues. Children here are parrots in the sense that they learn the dialogue by repeating after a model; however, they are encouraged to do so only after they understand the meaning of the dialogue. Dialogues for the parrot pairs game are taught by means of repetition, using the technique of Steinberg and Cazden's previously remarked upon "instructional chains." Peer models are first taught the dialogues by the teacher, and the peer models then teach these dialogues to their pairs.

In the "Parrot Pairs" game, peer models use natural forms of language to direct their pairs, but the speech learned in the dialogue is specific in the sense that it teaches particular language patterns; that is, specific patterns of speech as question forms, tense, pronouns, etc. The game gives children concentrated one-to-one tutoring on specific language forms as part of a structured play situation. The peer model first speaks the entire dialogue, using two puppets. He then permits the learner to choose the puppet whose part he wishes to speak. The chosen puppet's part of the dialogue is then taught to the learner by the model through prompting and repetition. The learner repeats after the model and obtains corrective feedback. The learner also must be aware of cues from the model that signal his puppet's turn to speak. When once the dialogues are learned, they are presented with the puppets before the class.

Holley and King (1972) did a study on second-language learning and found that individual modeling with pairs learning dialogues together was an effective teaching procedure. Children enjoy dialogues and learn language forms by speaking words given to a puppet. A game of parrot pairs makes learning language a dual communication process. The game incorporates the natural learning strategy of Peer Prompting because it includes imitation, repetition, and peer teaching.

The fact that children are quite eager and pleased to participate in the peer-pair teaching format is revealed by the spontaneous rhyme chanted by a first-grade peer model teaching a second-language learner the color words through the game of color bingo.

> One, two—
> I am one, you are two.
> I will teach some words to you,
> Color words like red, white, and blue.
> I will teach these words to you.

The natural strategy of Peer Prompting that children apply to the learning of a second language can be put into action in a classroom where children learn language from peers in both spontaneous and patterned social interaction.

Painting a Story

Miguel and María are enthusiastically wielding their paintbrushes at their easels. Miguel has created a formidable monster. The ferociousness of the beast is captured as Miguel adds the final touch—a set of bright red brush strokes to symbolize the fire which is flaring out through the monster's nostrils.

María is standing beside her picture, sending it admiring glances. Obviously pleased with her accomplishment, she proudly announces to Miguel that she has finished. Miguel scrutinizes María's painting. The large woman who dominates the scene catches Miguel's attention. Pointing to the figure, he asks María who the woman is. María, happy to be asked, proceeds to tell Miguel the story she painted into the picture.

Miguel: (Pointing to figure in María's painting) ¿Quién es ella?
(Who is she?)

María: Es la mamá. (She is the mother.)

Miguel: ¿Qué está haciendo? (What's she doing?)

María: Los niños regresan a la casa. La mama está en la puerta esperándoles. La mamá dice a la niña: "¡Mi gordita! ¿Pasaste un buen diá en la escuela? ¿Qué hiciste?" Los niños entran a la casa. La abuelita está mirando una novela en la televisión. La bebita está comiendo unos buñuelos. La niña pregunta a la abuelita: "¿Pasó un buen día?" La abuelita es una viejita y está muy arrugada, pero es muy amable. Los niños la quieren mucho. Cuando una persona en la familia está enferma, la abuelita llama a un curandero. Ella siempre enciende las velas de los santos para pedir muchos favores para la familia y para que los fantasmas malos no entren en la casa cada noche.
(The children come home. The mother is at the door waiting for them. The mother says to the girl, "My darling! Did you have a good day in school? What did you do?" The children go into the house. The grandmother is watching a soap opera on television. The baby is eating fried Mexican pastry. The girl asks the grandmother, "Did you have a good day?" The grandmother is an old lady and is very wrinkled, but is very nice. The children love her very much. When someone in the family is sick, the grandmother calls a healer. She always lights candles to the saints to ask for blessings for the family so that the bad spirits (ghosts) will not enter the house each night.)

(Bobby joins María and Miguel. Bobby is María's English-speaking friend from school.)

Bobby: (Pointing) Who's that? Tell me the story!

María: This is a house.
          This is a tree.
          The kids go home.
          They do their homework.
          The mother is making hot dogs for dinner.

BILINGUAL-BICULTURAL STRATEGY
AND SECOND-LANGUAGE LEARNING
WEARING TWO HATS

The scenario María recreates for Miguel in Spanish is more than a description of her painting. It is a cultural portrayal of her family life which is understood by Miguel as a speaker of the language and as a member of the culture. This shared understanding provides the backdrop against which María paints a verbal picture in Spanish of family members whose interactions are shaped by mutual bonds of affection as well as by a complex network of cultural beliefs and values.

When Bobby, María's English-speaking friend, requests information about the painting, María immediately switches to English, the language Bobby knows best. María describes her painting to him by alluding to terms associated with the American culture, such as "hot dogs." This changing of language code and culture is depicted symbolically by María's removal of the sombrero (representative of the Mexican culture) to reveal an American baseball cap. The strategy of switching to the language that the listener knows best in order to convey cultural, social meaning is labeled **Wearing Two Hats.**

As children master English as a second language, they acquire more than another linguistic code—they acquire a second culture. Sapir (1947) defines culture as the "socially inherited assemblage of practices and beliefs." Pelto and Pelto (1966) state that culture is related to thought processes and behavior. It is:

> . . . a total lifeway, not just a superficial set of customs. It largely shapes how man feels, behaves, and perceives as he adapts to his world. It is a dynamic process of interaction between persons within a specified environment in which their values and belief systems influence their perception of and reaction to life situations.

Children begin the process of acquiring a second culture by adopting a set of verbal and nonverbal behaviors which have a shared cultural group identification. Group solidarity is reinforced through conventional expressions and referents. Children learn such words and expressions as a systematized set of vocal habits appropriate to various social settings. The results of becoming knowledgeable in the second language and culture, combined with first language proficiency, is that children become functional members of two social, cultural groups. They become bilingual and bicultural. They employ the strategy of Wearing Two Hats to distinguish between their dual social identities. Children switch languages to express differently coded social relationships. Language is intricately woven into the fabric of each "hat" and becomes an important and powerful social tool for expressing interpersonal and intergroup intentions and motivations. Language switching then assumes a direct relationship between the social situation and the speaker's relation to the listener.

Children who are most capable of putting into practice the Wearing Two Hats strategy have internalized the following for each language: first, a sense of personal identity; second, social situational meaning; third, cultural attitudes and values; fourth, emotional and psychological factors; and finally, linguistic flexibility.

The first factor, establishing a sense of identity in each language, involves integrating socially significant features of environment and culture. There is no simple one-to-one relationship between specific speech codes and specific identities (Blom and Gumperz 1960). This fact can be explained by considering how language codes are learned. The first language is acquired at home in the atmosphere of intimate domestic and close friendship relationships. The second language, on the other hand, is learned in school in a more standardized, formal presentation. The initial acquisition patterns of the first and second language influence the cultural identities adopted by children. The extent to which cultural identities may be labeled "distinct" is directly related to the role of language in socialization practices.

The fundamental base of the child's first cultural identity is established through familial socialization before he or she enters school. Contextualized speech develops as a natural part of the socialization process in the home where communication proceeds against shared background knowledge (Ervin-Tripp 1977). Children learn terms to communicate intimacy, solidarity, and distance. They learn to utilize familiar and polite language forms through role relationships within the home. Cultural identity based on language usage is reinforced not only within the home, but extends to the ethnic community. Cultural expressions learned in the home are reinforced in the ethnic community through social encounters. María communicates about her painting to Miguel through individual expressions which are identified with their common culture. She uses terms of endearment such as, "mi gordita," to express the close ties which exist between mother and child. She quotes conversations between family members using the familiar and the polite forms to delineate role relationships. The mother addresses the children in the familiar "tu" form, while the child addresses the grandmother in the polite or formal "usted" form of the language. The child shows respect for the grandmother by using the polite form. María is confident Miguel, with whom she shares a significant cultural identity, understands the implied social implications of speaking in polite versus informal forms. Thus, the elaborate narrative María relates to Miguel progresses as a relaxed conversation between intimates.

María's conversation in English with Bobby, on the other hand, is marked by its factual brevity and its emotional restraint, both factors indicative of the less assured cultural identity which exists between the two children. María uses sentences to describe her painting that sound like an English as a second-language lesson: "This is a house. This is a tree." María's language does not reflect the fact that she is one of the most fluent English speakers in the class and is reading on the third-grade level. She nonverbally exhibits no outward signs of emotion as she replies to Bobby. This is in direct contrast to the vivacity and emotionalism that characterize her interaction with Miguel.

María's linguistic behavior can in part be interpreted as a manifestation of the school socialization process which has molded her language and second cultural identity. While the socialization experience of the home has relied on shared meaning defined by intimate social relationships, the school experience is based on standardized forms associated with receiving and giving instructions for formal classroom activities. Thus, the school socialization experience is necessarily discontinuous with that of the home in certain important respects. Although the basic universal features of realizing meaning from others' speech remain similar, formal schooling must need be a shift away from the expectation of shared assumptions (Ervin-Tripp 1977). Much of the school socialization experience depends on attending to specific instructional settings. Language in the classroom is associated with formal subject matter rather than with informal social interaction. Children learn to express themselves in English in the context of an academic activity. The teacher uses language to shape and direct the structure of the activity to an academic end.

Another significant difference between home and school socialization experiences is the emphasis placed on communicating on an emotional or personal level. The personal, emotional aspects of the language which are emphasized in the home culture are seldom reinforced by the school (Gonzalez 1977). Pinnell (1975) confirmed this observation in her study of the language used in most classrooms. She found that only 5% of the statements used in classrooms could be classified as personal language. Pinnell states:

> Teachers seemed to operate in accordance with what they saw as their major task, helping children to develop skills and accumulate knowledge and communicated this expectation to students. At the same time they communicated a high value for work-related talk or for answers. Children seemed to sense that value and limited themselves to work-related language.

This preference for work-related language in the school setting may be interpreted by second-language learners as an indication that personal feelings are not important or proper topics for conversation within the school setting. Personal feelings are associated with the first language. The second language is limited to the expression of factual statements. A dichotomy is thus established between the two communication codes whereby the languages remain segregated by functional usage which is defined by children's socialization experiences. Children therefore express meaning differently in each language. They establish dual ethnic identities.

Lambert (1972) believes that dual identities arise in bilingual children because the meaning systems of the two languages are inherently irreconcilable. Bilingual children internalize two systems of meaning. They carry two different structures of reality in their heads. This is consistent with the Whorfian hypothesis which states that language structures one's views of reality. Children learn systems of social meaning which are consistent with the world view they hold for each language.

Learning social meaning is the second factor which establishes the Wearing Two Hats strategy as a communication tool. Conversational inference can occur with speakers of the same language simply because they agree upon a certain level of social interpretation.

> Conversational inference depends on shared social presuppositions and if conversational continuity is a function of the success of such inferences then the mere fact that two speakers can sustain an interaction over time is evidence for the existence of at least some common level of social knowledge and agreement on interpretation (Gumperz and Herasimchuk 1972).

This shared social interpretation is the foundation upon which children build to sustain dialogue. Terms are often unique to a social network and meaningful only in a culturally related context. María's narration includes various words and expressions which are understood fully only by another member of the Mexican culture. María informs Miguel that when anyone in her family is sick the grandmother calls a "curandero." The direct translation of this word may be "a healer," but the real meaning of the word "curandero" is understood only within the culture. The curandero is someone called upon in the Hispanic culture to treat the sick. He or she is highly respected for possessing the unique knowledge to cure the sick. Curanderos use herbs, prayers, and oils as treatments. The concept of the curandero is strongly rooted in the Hispanic culture, just as the concept of the medical doctor is a part of the American culture. María does not mention the curandero when describing her picture to Bobby because as an "outsider" to the Mexican culture the word would have no meaning for him. So, also, she doesn't mention that the baby is eating buñelos in her English rendition of the story. María is aware that effective communication is based on shared social meaning. Knowing two languages is not a simple matter of duplication; it is linguistic competence based on differential social, cultural experiences.

María switches language codes and social arenas as she addresses Bobby. María thus redefines the social interaction. María's English version of the story includes the statement, "The mother is making hot dogs for dinner." María's inclusion of this reference to the American culture reveals her desire to socially adapt her speech to convey meaning to Bobby. Gumperz and Hernandez (1972) speak of code-switching which speakers use as a verbal strategy in much the same way as authors switch styles in a story. Styles are switched to change emphasis or topics. Codes are switched to emphasize social meaning.

The strategy of code-switching is usually done spontaneously. It can be the conscious or unconscious selection of different variants depending in part on who is listening. The strategy is illustrative of the way children adapt their speech to the requirements of the addressees. Those who have studied language choices of children agree that they make their choice of code depending on the primary language of their listeners. Genishi (1976) studied four Chicano six-year-olds in a kindergarten day-care center and found that the only variable that had a clear effect on language choice was the linguistic ability of the listener. Zentella (1978) investigated older Puerto Rican children in the third and sixth grades. Zentella's results support those of Geneshi in that children were noted to switch languages to accommodate to the addressee. Children demonstrate their sociolinguistic competence and bicultural identities through their ability to switch language codes.

Switching language codes signifies social distance as well as social rapport and proximity. The concept of social distance has been used mainly to refer to the degree of separation which exists between participants in a conversation (Scotten and Ury 1977). Where identification is strong, the social distance between individuals is small. Speech occurs in a social context of familiarity and shared meaning; the attributes of persons or objects are less likely to be specified. María's conversation with Miguel is characterized as casual speech. Identification between them is strong; they share an ethnic identity. Labov (1966) did extensive work on the role of ethnic identity of speaker and language. He noted a more casual style of speech among speakers who share the same family or ethnic background. Weak boundaries of social distance exist between children who have been participants in the same system of socialization in their preschool years.

María's switch to English to communicate with Bobby may be understood as a symbol of increased social distance. Their contact has been at the school in a rather impersonal, academic atmosphere. Rubin (1968) states that relationships of social distance may be signaled by switching between distinct languages. The socialization experience the child has had in a language, then, will determine what language the child will speak, to whom he or she will speak it, in what social context, and on which level of social intimacy.

The third factor of the Wearing Two Hats strategy explores the social meaning of language in terms of cultural beliefs, attitudes, and values. Beliefs and values are learned by children through participation in family affairs and cultural rituals. Culture is represented linguistically by a speech community which proliferates vocabulary around things and events of great concern to it (Hymes 1970). Speech acts rest on mutually shared beliefs. María talks about cultural beliefs with Miguel. She uses their cultural bond to enrich the content of the message. A belief of the Hispanic culture is that females are expected to provide emotional and spiritual support for the family. This keeps the concept of the "familia," or extended family, alive and functional (Ramirez and Castaneda 1974). María refers to this concept of the extended family in her dialogue with Miguel as she talks about the grandmother and the children's love for her. María relies upon Miguel's knowledge of the culture as she describes the rituals the grandmother performs to keep away evil spirits. The lighting of candles is an ethnic belief which María has embedded deep in her imagination. The richness of the word "fantasmas" (ghosts, spirits) can only be understood as part of a total cultural experience. Therefore, the word cannot be translated effectively to convey its full significance. Rubin (1968) further illustrates this point by stating that "linguistic representation may be quite constant across individuals in a given culture; the meanings of messages will reflect the idiosyncrasies of that cultural experience." Thus, to fully understand the language, one must be privy to the culture.

Concepts of various beliefs are shaped by the culture and manifested through the language. María narrates a story to Miguel which implies religious beliefs such as the grandmother's asking for blessings for the family. Superstitious beliefs also can contribute to the culture and to the language. Thus, the cultural beliefs to which the child is exposed defines what he or she knows or feels about the world. Culture may be defined as the totality of habits shared by members of a society as a "general method of behavior by which they organize their life from cradle to the grave" (Sommer 1974). Culture embraces all aspects of shared life within the family and community. There are countless behaviors, habits, beliefs, and attitudes that are assimilated by the child through exposure to the culture before he or she enters school.

School entrance for the second-language learner marks the beginning of a new cultural experience both linguistically and socially. The process of schooling for the second-language learner is a communicative process not only in the traditional sense of transmitting knowledge, but also in the sense of imparting a second culture. The sociocultural experience of academia may impart to the child a set of attitudes and values that are quite different from those which have composed his or her primary socialization experience. María's rendition of the story to Bobby includes the statement, "They do their homework." Homework is a tradition of the school environment. The tradition also reflects an American cultural value of academic achievement. Coupled with academic achievement is the belief in individual competition. This belief may be very different for children who have been socialized in their first culture to consider self-interests secondary to those of the family group. Children must learn and assimilate a new set of cultural values and beliefs.

Children, as Miguel and María, are ultimately socialized in two systems, the home and the school. They must learn to function in two cultural worlds by assuming a bicultural identity. Bicultural is defined by Webster as the "existence of two distinct cultures." Becoming bicultural includes learning culturally unique preferred modes of relating to others behaviorally and linguistically.

Children who are bicultural have learned that linguistic forms and behavior are not everywhere equivalent in communicative role and cultural value. The matching of culture values to linguistic expression underlies children's ability to communicate in two social worlds. The home language and the school language remain separate because of the children's efforts to maintain a sense of integrity in each culture. Malherbe (1943) sums up how social situational factors influence children's expression by saying, "It is doubtful whether bilingualism per se can be measured apart from the situation it is to function in." Thus, children vary their language production according to the particular purpose the language serves in the social environment.

The social purpose of language takes on even broader significance when its likely psychological consequences are contemplated. How precisely language influences emotional adjustment and personality is the fourth factor revealed in children's use of the Wearing Two Hats strategy. Children are initially taught language by their mothers, the key socialization figure in the home. The psychological closeness that exists between mother and child enables him or her to interpret the mother's words through the overt affection she displays. Feelings, attitudes, troubles, and joys are labeled by the child in response to social interaction with family and community members. The extreme relevance of these childhood experiences on personality development and behavior has been verified by many psychologists. Language has been termed a powerful reinforcer of behavior. This is especially true of the language children learn at home which is closely tied to initial emotional experiences. Parents' positive or negative verbal responses to children's actions affect their behavior as well as affirm or negate their self-concepts. The home milieu to which children have been exposed contributes to the development of their personality. Children's social observations and partialities are a reflection of their home life (Coles 1967). This means that children have the strong inclination to reflect their parents' views in their own speech and behavior. The associations children have formed in their minds are manifested in their language. Children have learned to communicate human emotions and factual information in their first language through social encounters. Children feel comfortable when talking about something that catches their attention, troubles them or makes them happy.

Psychologically, school entrance has a profound impact on children who speak little or no English. The sterility that is encountered in some strict classroom routines creates a dichotomy in children's interpretation of the function of the second language. Children come to believe that they must articulate only factual material in the second language and continue to rely on their first language to discuss and impart sentiments. This linguistic compartmentalization is often observed as second-language learners congregate with those who speak their first language on the playground. Social interactions are simply more comfortable in the first language where children can assume receptivity and understanding not only linguistically but attitudinally. María's commentary on her painting to Miguel and then to Bobby illustrates the duality between a personal versus a factual explanation. María's behavior may reflect the formality that characterizes the classroom procedures of instruction in the second language. One might suppose that María has had little opportunity to interact personally with second-language speakers in the classroom setting.

The ability to articulate feelings in a second language enables children to perceive a sense of psychological rapport with the culture. When a person experiences a culture psychologically, his or her whole being is involved— emotions and intellect. Sharing social experiences is critical to the development of ease of expression. The understanding which arises from this involvement and participation in the culture can never be duplicated by intellectual knowledge alone. To experience another culture is to touch, feel, and respond emotionally to others who are members of that culture. Purely intellectual knowledge of a culture and language does not necessarily promote personal affiliation. It is imperative that the teacher create opportunities for children to strengthen bonds with the second culture through active social participation with peers on a personal as well as on an academic basis.

The teacher serves as a model for personalized use of the second language by communicating with children about their feelings. Children learn language not only through the teacher's direct instruction of subject matter in English, but more importantly psychologically by the way the teacher expresses positive or negative approval of them. The teacher who communicates positive feelings to children in the second language makes it easy for them to learn to do likewise. The teacher also contributes positively to children's personality development by positively affirming children's intellectual as well as personal and social capabilities. Children become comfortable in the second language as they develop rapport with the teacher and peers through personal interactions. As a consequence of this rapport, children assimilate academic and personal ways of speaking in the second language into a complete system of communication. They no longer must change hats to comment factually or express themselves emotionally. They can begin to cultivate linguistic flexibility.

It is this linguistic flexibility which is the final component of the Wearing Two Hats strategy which enriches children's communicative competence to enable them to use both languages for all social functions. These functions include: establishing and maintaining social relations, expressing their feelings and reactions, hiding intentions, seeking and giving information, talking one's way out of trouble, learning or teaching how to make something, conversing over the telephone, problem solving, discussing ideas, playing with language, and acting out social roles (Rivers and Temperly 1978). The extent to which children can bring these functions to bear on social situations may be thought of as their communicative linguistic repertoire (Gumperz 1964). Bernstein (1961) has described this communicative repertoire as the verbal process through which actors select from a range of alternatives that are appropriate in varying interpersonal encounters. Becoming bilingual and feeling equally comfortable in two cultures is an outcome of mastering these functions and overcoming any feelings of alienation.

Linguistic flexibility must be evaluated against the environment in which children function both linguistically and socially. The linguistic dimension pays attention to children's ability to communicate using all previously mentioned functions (repertoire) in both languages, while the social dimension concerns itself with their bicultural status and the ease with which they adapt to various social roles.

To sum up the discussion, Wearing Two Hats is a multidimensional strategy for conveying meaning in two linguistic systems. It involves more than code-switching or changing languages to conform to the system the listener knows best. The strategy encompasses establishing two cultural identities which make it possible to: understand social situational meaning, communicate using cultural linguistic patterns and group identity expressions, establish a sense of rapport psychologically and emotionally through association with cultural attitudes and values, and ultimately develop functional linguistic flexibility to the extent that it becomes an unconscious process.

Bilingual children wear two hats and change them to appropriately dress for the occasion. This change of hats, as is usual with a change of apparel, brings with it some change of feelings to the personality. The bilingual child operates on two levels of feeling and must be comfortable on both levels. The two hats, although different in style, are still of the same genus "hat." The Wearing Two Hats strategy appreciates the "different" while stressing the "same," making a bilingual child fluent in both languages and integrated in the cultures of both languages—different but the same—Wearing Two Hats with the plume of pride decorating each hat.

IMPLICATIONS OF WEARING TWO HATS FOR SECOND-LANGUAGE LEARNING AND CLASSROOM TEACHING

Bilingual-bicultural children who can comfortably and appropriately "change hats" are products of an educational system where attention is given to experience-based training as well as to the imparting of intellectual knowledge. It follows that the teacher's role is all important. Students often are successful to the degree that the teacher can select and implement productive teaching strategies. Although the quality of instruction is synonymous with the teacher's effectiveness, the latter often is dependent upon how bilingual education is defined and the model which is adhered to in a particular school system. The U. S. Office of Education defines bilingual education as:

> The use of two languages, one of which is English, as mediums of instruction for the same pupil population in a well organized program which encompasses part of the curriculum and includes the history and cultural associations with the mother tongue. A complete program develops and maintains the children's self-esteem and pride in both cultures.

This definition has been translated into various models of bilingual education. Two of these are maintenance and transitional programs. In maintenance programs equal importance is given to the first and second language and culture. Transitional programs use the native language only temporarily as a bridge to English instruction. In actual practice, these programs are implemented in the following ways:

1. The self-contained classroom. One bilingual teacher is assisted by a bilingual aide.
2. Team-teaching. Two teachers, one bilingual and one monolingual, pool their teaching strengths.
3. The integrated full-day program. Pupils from different classes are "pulled out" and given special instruction in subjects by a bilingual teacher.
4. The department model. Students receive instruction in subjects from different bilingual teachers in different rooms. Integration with other students is essential.
5. A non-bilingual teacher is assisted by a bilingual aide.
6. A district-wide center for newly arrived non-English speaking pupils.

The variety of models confirms the fact that no one approach is satisfactory for all school districts. The number of bilingual students and the district's philosophy of bilingual education often determine the basic approach taken. The emphasis, however, is placed on the model rather than on learning or teaching variables that should be part of a successful bilingual program. There is usually only a minimum of direction given to teachers. There are no common goals and objectives for all bilingual programs. Yet the needs to learn English, the problems of cultural adjustment, the frustrations, and the search for identity are universal to all non-English speakers in these programs.

It appears, therefore, that a different kind of framework in the approach to bilingual-bicultural education should be considered. This framework should be multidimensional and designed specifically to meet the needs of children who all their lives "wear two hats." Children in bilingual or ESL programs often develop fragmented language skills because all facets of learning are not integrated. Language and culture are separated. English is taught with concentration on reading and writing skills, disregarding cultural awareness. Even the first language is taught only as an academic bridge to learning rather than as an integral part of a culture's lifestyle. Language and culture, however, in actuality are inseparable; to teach one implies teaching the other. Comprehension of the culture is essential for effective language communication.

In contrast to the fragmented approach of teaching language apart from the culture, a multidimensional integrated approach would enrich language with culture through simultaneous social experiential learning and interdisciplinary subject-matter presentation. This model categorizes student-learning in three dimensions: cognitive, affective, and social action. The two main instructional variables are: presentation and opportunity for social interaction.

The correlation of the instructional variables to student-learning dimensions is the key to effective implementation of the multidimensional model. The first dimension to be considered within the multidimensional framework is the cognitive. Under cognition there are the following subtypes: information, analysis, synthesis, comprehension, and insight (Kleinjans 1975). Information deals with encyclopedia-type facts—persons, places, events, and dates. Analysis separates parts of a concept, such as a family system. Synthesis integrates the meaningful relationships of the parts. Whereas synthesis is concerned with facts or existing elements, comprehension is concerned with new items or predicting from the facts according to a cultural viewpoint and drawing insight from the accumulated understanding.

An example of how these subtypes of cognition would be integrated is in the study of famous cultural personalities. Simón Bolívar is studied as a famous Hispanic figure, Lincoln as an important personage in the American culture. Each famous person is examined and researched in the language he spoke. A multidisciplinary approach to acquiring knowledge about each figure includes: social studies, math, reading, writing, and cultural viewpoints. In social studies, historical facts are surveyed. Factual material also is considered mathematically, i.e., the amount of money Bolívar or Lincoln needed to pay his army, the cost of supplies, means of raising amounts of money, etc. are discussed and computed. Reading skills draw children into making inferences about each man's behavior in relation to the times in which he lived, his personal goals and his commitment to the betterment of society. Conclusions reached by children then are synthesized in writing or in small group discussions. The fact that Bolívar paid his army from his personal funds poses various questions about his character and motives. Why was the revolution important to Bolívar? Advanced students can compare and contrast the Civil

War with Bolívar's unification plan in South America. Multidisciplinary lessons about important persons give children the opportunity to acquire cultural insight. This is the ability to not only look at a culture from the inside, but also to see the world outside as the people of the culture see it. The ability to observe the same phenomenon (such as war or revolutions) and interpret meaning from the viewpoints of two cultures is an achievement of the bicultural-bilingual individual.

Younger children can develop many of these cognitive skills. At first children can learn them orally in both languages before they learn to read, through listening activities that require comprehension. Visual aids, such as movies, filmstrips, and artwork, can also serve as teaching tools.

Cognitive learning is reinforced by the strategy the teacher uses for presentation of subject matter. By teaching about famous personalities in the language the children speak, the teacher can use a code-switching strategy. This code-switching strategy gives the teacher flexibility to use the two languages to teach cognitive skills in a nonredundant manner. Language choice becomes relevant to the extent to which the preference of one language over the other is significant and appropriate, according to the information to be taught.

The teacher also can take advantage of cues and plan lessons by building them into subject-matter presentation. Cues trigger alternation in languages. The teacher might be talking about the number "twelve" in English and cue a switch to Spanish by asking the question, "¿Y qué otra palabra puede usar en vez de doce y hablar de la misma cantidad?" (And what other word can you use instead of twelve to talk about the same quantity?) This question cues the children to switch "hats" and start thinking in Spanish.

The technique of eliciting lesson objectives by alternating languages throughout the day builds cognitive skills in both languages without redundant translation. It also establishes the equality of both languages. Hornby (1977) states, "It seems only when the status of the two languages is both high and relatively equal, and when both languages are spoken by individuals important to the child, that the child responds to the challenge of becoming bilingual." Children who become bilingual do so in an environment that fosters both languages.

The second instructional variable that must be applied to cognitive learning is the opportunity for social interaction. Small group instruction that enriches cognitive skills includes two types of activities which Rivers (1976) has termed "skill-getting and skill-using." In skill-getting, teachers structure group teaching lessons to introduce new vocabulary and grammatical patterns. Activities for skill-using are left largely unstructured. The focus is on giving children opportunities to communicate with each other and thus practice the skills learned in a way that is natural. The more opportunities children have to practice both languages in unstructured activities, the more proficient they will become in thinking in two languages and operating in two cultures.

Harmonious identification with both cultures is a stated goal in most recent bilingual education programs (Gonzalez 1977). Meaningful learning must take place on an affective as well as on a cognitive basis. Research indicates that the most successful second-language learning takes place when the learner feels he or she is gaining something rather than giving up something. This suggests that the child's first language and culture should be nurtured while the second language and culture are introduced as an additive process. Additive bilingualism contends that successful academic learning will take place only if care is taken of children's social and psychological needs, particularly as these relate to ethnic identity. Children have attitudes, values, and motivational patterns that are part of this identity and contribute to their self-concept. At the core of children's self-concept is the value which they attach to the language they speak. A rejection of children's first language and culture is like a rejection of the children themselves. Evidence from research concerning the self-concept among children indicates a tendency of children from ethnic minorities to make a negative evaluation of themselves, their skin color, and their culture. A negative self-concept has an adverse effect on school learning. Immersion of children into an all-English culture may contribute to a negative self-concept because it carries the implicit suggestion that their mother tongue is of inferior value and that bilingualism is an undesirable attribute. Psychological disturbances, such as withdrawal, submission, and segregation, may take place. Contrarily, a positive self-concept is promoted when children are encouraged to have respect for their culture and mother tongue. This encouragement would lead to a desirable self-image, better social and personal adjustment, and increased ability to profit from the school experiences.

It is the task of the school, therefore, to aid children to integrate and synthesize a new language and culture while allowing them to retain identity with their own ethnic group. The goal of the school is to promote bicultural functioning. In a democratic environment where one culture is not valued over another this goal can become a reality.

A study conducted by Goebes and Shore (1978) confirmed the general hypothesis that a bicultural school environment has a significant positive effect on the personality development of children. When children in a bicultural school environment were compared to those in a monocultural school, the following factors were noted:

1. more heterogeneous peer group structure

2. better self-image

3. greater acceptance of culture differences

4. better ability to take different cultural roles

These factors are all significant in the second category of student learning, the affective domain. Bicultural identity is fostered through affective as well as through cognitive learning. There are five levels in the affective domain that affect children's achieving a bicultural identity. These are: admiration, comprehension, association, familiarization and assessment. Admiration simply refers to children coming to know and like aspects of both cultures, including food and music as well as aesthetic and moral values. Comprehension involves learning to understand and accept why people in each culture behave the way they do. Association is learning to become one with the people of the two cultures. Familiarization means participating in the customs of two cultures and sharing their values. Assessment is the process of evaluating the values of both cultures; this might mean shifting priorities, giving up certain values for new ones, or enlarging one's value system to include values from both cultures.

The teacher promotes affective learning by presenting customs of both cultures in planned activities. Stories, art work, and holidays of each culture contribute to affective learning. Perhaps most important is the teacher's sensitivity to each culture enabling him or her to construct affective learning experiences for children.

Social interaction in the affective domain is established in an emotionally supportive environment. Here, once again, the teacher's sensitivity is very important. Teachers must be able to recognize the diversity of child socialization practices which affect personality. Hispanic children may be more highy motivated in group settings cordial to their stronger affiliation needs and greater desires to belong to a social group (Ramirez and Castaneda 1974). The teacher can build on this predisposition by structuring group activities which encourage children to interact with one another in both languages. Children feel free to develop a bicultural identity when they observe the teacher and other children interacting with one another in the two languages without any observable preference for either one, except where context appropriateness may suggest.

Affective factors are not only nourished in group settings, but also on a one-to-one basis. Talking informally to students and having spontaneous conversations with children about personal matters and feelings have many positive benefits. They affirm children's self-worth by encouraging them to communicate about something which they, themselves, consider significant and express values they see as important, while having someone important, as the teacher, who cares enough to pay attention to what they have to say. Even in the best of educational situations, encouragement for discussion and an array of materials are not sufficient. How the teacher subtly communicates with children is what makes the critical difference in the school's contribution to the child's affective learning. Thus, the teacher's instructional goal in the affective domain is to help children experience in the classroom all levels of affective learning that will contribute to the children's feelings of worth. Such positive feelings take shape when the children experience that what they think, feel, and value makes a difference in interpersonal relations.

The multidimensional framework for bilingual-bicultural education has one final area—social-action learning. This aspect of learning includes learning social functions of language and assuming social roles. The social functions of language comprise all those instances where communication serves a social function, such as recreational and religious activities. The focus here is on social factors which affect the structure of language in contact and social use. Each culture will have unique group expressions and characteristic modes of meaning which can be acquired only through participation in the speech community.

Assuming social roles in each culture results from multilearning experiences in school, at home, and in the community. Rules of social interaction and language usage are learned along with social-cultural roles. For example, the children's social role in the Hispanic community is to defer to elders behaviorally and linguistically by using the polite form of Spanish with them. The social role of a friend calls for informal behavior and language. Children learn various ways of speaking that reflect these roles. They become productive members of society by integrating a number of roles into their personalities.

The teacher's role in social-action learning is to prepare students to participate in society. To do this he or she must become involved in the community where students live and relate this to the wider community. The teacher must coalesce school learning with real-world experiences. Teachers, to do this, must understand how the community thinks, what behavior they expect from children at home and in the neighborhood, and which role they expect the school to play in teaching their children. Understanding promotes a unification of goals so that the school and the community are not working at cross-purposes.

To conclude the chapter on the strategy of Wearing Two Hats, it may be said that the strategy is best developed in a multidimensional bilingual-bicultural educational model where the teacher strives through the techniques of effective presentation of subject-matter and proliferation of opportunities for social interaction to nourish and integrate the three types of student learning: cognitive, affective, and social-action. Educational outcomes in this model are explained as a function of interaction between children's background culture, second culture, and educational treatment, factors that allow for synthesis and integration. The goal of this synthesis is to expand linguistic and mental flexibility. This flexibility includes a fusion of all the elements from each culture, not as a dualism but as a combination that allows children to function easily and comfortably in two cultural worlds. It allows them to transcend the insularity of the monolingual's world and gives them the flexibility to interrelate cultural factors for creative language use for a full life of communication on a cognitive and feeling level. Bilingual-bicultural citizens are a resource our country can fully tap, with the cream of cross-cultures rising to the top of creativity.

I'm the Teacher

It is "choosing time" in the classroom. Students select the activity they will pursue for the next twenty minutes. Miguel and María decide to explore the boxes in the role-play corner of the classroom. Boxes contain different costumes and props. María chooses a box filled with adult clothing. She pulls out some high heels and a curly wig. She looks intently at the wig as if trying to place where she has seen it before. She then glances at the curly-haired teacher. A big smile comes over María's face as she understands the connection. She places the wig on her head, puts on a long dress along with the high-heeled shoes and announces to Miguel, "I'm the teacher." She hands Miguel a small chalk-board and proceeds to role-play the teacher. Later, the children reverse roles and Miguel acts out his interpretation of the teacher.

María: I'm the teacher.
          The teacher's smart.
          The teacher does pluses.
          How much is 7 + 2?

Miguel: So easy! Nine!

María: Nice job.
          How much is 7 + 2 + 3?

Miguel: Eleven.

María: No, not a good job!
          I'm going to teach you.
          Count seven, now two, now three.
          Do it!

Miguel: That's ten.

María: How'd you do that?
          You keep getting it wrong!
          I'll show you. See? Look! Listen!

Miguel: Yea, oh I know it, twelve!

María: Very nice job.
          Now a hard one—7 + 2 + 3 + 4.

Miguel: So easy—sixteen!

María: You smartie head—I'm going to give you an animal sticker.

Miguel: Now, I'm the teacher.
        Put two fingers up.
        Now put three more.
        Now count.

María: No fingers. See!
        I know, I know, five.

Miguel: Sit down! Pick up the paper!

María: No, I don't wanna.

Miguel: Well, you hafta! You on report!
        I'm very mad at you!
        You gonna stay after!

María: No, I'm not.

Miguel: I want you right down the office—right now! (motioning as if to
        another student) Bring this kid down the office.

María: Teacher's always pickin' on girls.

ROLE-PLAYING STRATEGY
AND SECOND-LANGUAGE LEARNING
COPYCATTING

Once upon a learning of English as a second language, two children, Miguel and María, affectively acted out the role of the teacher . . . and they spoke expressively ever after. Learning the second language through affective imitation in role-play can be termed **Copycatting.** This strategy allows children to transform themselves into another person during pretend play by verbally and motorically copying their perception of the behavior. Copycatting is further defined as an affective, selective, individual, creative, and social process of imitation. It is affective in that feelings of the person are copied through verbal and nonverbal patterns. Selective imitation is manifested as children choose what to copy of the model's behavior and actions. Individuality expresses the fact that a commonly experienced event will be imitated differently by children. Individual perceptions of social realities are delineated in enactments. Creativity is expressed through dialogue elaboration. Socially, the strategy permits the matching of imitated grammar used by the model with spontaneous social expressions in a natural, conversational context. These forms of imitation are practiced by children during role-play to develop the second language.

Considerable research suggests a role for imitation in the development of language or communication skills, but actual role-playing as one form of learning a second language has not been specifically studied (Whitehurst and Vasta 1975). Therefore, the strategy of Copycatting is presented in this chapter to illustrate how children join together the natural pair, acting and conversation, to acquire communicative competence in English.

Children initially learn language by tying words to actions. Language is learned in the context of a social situation. It is part of a larger behavioral unit which consists of both verbal and nonverbal elements. Affective imitation in role-play brings together both these elements. During role-play, children mimic facial expressions, gestures, and posture along with words. Miguel imitates the teacher's posture by putting his hands on his hips in an authoritarian manner. He furrows his brow as he becomes angry to signify his disapproval. María gestures toward the board as she explains a math problem to Miguel. Miguel and María thus learn to communicate in the second language through copying a wide variety of body language, including stance, gestures, etc. These nonverbal mannerisms give added meaning to words.

Copycatting through affective imitation also involves acting out emotions from the point of view of the model. Spoken words take on a definite tone. Miguel responds to María's refusal to sit down by taking on a commanding tone. He disciplines María, saying, "You on report! You gonna stay after! I want you right down the office!" María's explanation of math problems to Miguel sounds very pedantic: "I'll show you. See? Look! Listen!" When Miguel gives the wrong answer to the math problem, anger is noted in her voice. She says, "No, not a good job!" As Miguel repeatedly gives incorrect responses, María's voice conveys a sense of impatience: "How'd you do that?" An exasperated tone can be detected in María's statement, "You keep getting it wrong!" Finally, Miguel gets the right answer and María's comment takes on a happy note. She positively reinforces Miguel: "Very nice job." Miguel and María capture the emotional essence of the teacher's language. As they portray the teacher's role, they integrate verbal expressions with affective connotations.

Empathy as a factor in language learning is crucial in developing the affective use of the second language (Guiora 1972). Affect is developed as students climb into a new skin, becoming the person they are playing rather than maintaining the distance of pretend. Characterizing a model in a social context causes students to actively empathize with the role. This empathy permits English words to be mastered on a feeling level. By scripting English role models accurately, students gain a deep sensitivity to how feelings are differentially expressed. Children eventually obtain affective mastery of the second language through the repeated process of observing English language models around them, and imitating language expressively by throwing themselves wholeheartedly into role-play.

The second component of the Copycatting strategy is selective imitation. Second-language learning from this perspective is an active, flexible, and responsible process. Flexibility refers to the freedom children have to choose the language they will imitate during role-play. This permits them to express themselves with minimal inhibition regardless of their proficiency in English. This flexibility is noted as Miguel and María role-play the teacher. María appears to have better control over English language structures. She is able to replicate the teacher's sentences. Miguel has difficulty copying sentences. He copies the teacher's phrases leaving out words (I want you right down the office.) and inserting peer expressions such as "gonna" and "hafta."

Flexibility is also revealed in the variety of themes children portray through role-play. Thematic content refers to the behaviors portrayed in associations with a specific role and the nature of the interactions among role players (Curry and Arnaud 1974). The thematic content of Miguel and María's role-play was a math lesson. However, the teacher's behavior during the math lesson was selectively imitated by the children. María didactically chooses to imitate the teacher's explanatory language. María has probably heard the teacher say the same phrases many times during math instruction. María thus imitates: "Count two, now two more, now three." Miguel scripts the teacher as a disciplinarian who will take no nonsense. María's flip remark to Miguel, "I don't wanna," is followed by his adamant statement, "Well, you hafta!" The authoritarian theme Miguel selected probably was influenced by the role

María assumed as recalcitrant student. Throughout the dialogue in the role-play, the children selectively imitated the teacher's phrases to conform to the sociodrama they were enacting.

The themes children choose for role-play are related to the paramount emotional and social concerns of the age group (Curry and Arnaud 1974). Very young children role-play domestic and classroom themes. Older children enact social themes and ultrafeminine or masculine roles. While there seem to be some basic developmental regularities to these themes, children do bring some of their specific interests to act out in role-play. Children choose to imitate the role models with which they have an affinity or interest. They closely watch and listen to models, extracting the language which they will later copy in role-play. Miguel and María's portrayal of the teacher reveals the close attention they have paid to their teacher's language in the classroom. María's remarks to Miguel as she explains the math lesson have definite features of the teacher-talk register and more generally characterize the expression of someone in authority. María's directions to Miguel are punctuated by the attentional markers that teachers generally use: "See? Look! Listen!" Miguel mimics the way the teacher typically expresses displeasure in the form of a personal message. He says to María, "I'm very mad at you!" By capturing in their dialogue some exact copies of the teacher's words, Miguel and María also reveal an acute interest in the teacher's role. Roles of interest vitally engage the attention of children and direct them to take responsibility for arranging practice situations in the second language through role-play.

Responsibility is further actualized as students decide how they will practice English in the role-play format. Making decisions on language usage encourages children to become more confident second-language learners. Confidence develops as children feel free to select the language they will speak to portray an agreed upon theme. Role-playing is thus viewed as a language learning strategy through which children actively decide to copycat specific elements of speech, selecting their words and phrases to fit the context of a dramatic improvisation.

The third component of Copycatting may be described as an individualistic, creative strategy. Individualism refers to the style or manner in which children expressively portray their conception of the role. Role-play begins for second-language learners as simple, concrete imitation of perceived actions and their accompanied words. Later, children rearrange words and creatively add phrases learned from their own direct, social interactions in English. This process is referred to as "creative elaboration" of the role. Creative elaboration is expressed in a role-play dialogue through combinations and additions of social phrases to an otherwise literal imitation of a model. María creatively elaborates with the social expression, "You smartie head." This verbalization is not a direct imitation of the teacher's language but it fits the context of the role-play and expresses María's individual interpretation of the teacher's role.

Throughout the dialogue, María asserts the teacher's role and status as holder of "special knowledge" which must be imparted to students. She gives positive and negative feedback to Miguel in terms of how he grasps this "knowledge." Miguel's individual approach in portraying the role of student is very relaxed. His continued response is, "So easy." When roles are reversed and María becomes the student, she develops the role of a precocious, difficult child. She once again creatively elaborates on the student's role when in response to Miguel's ultimatum for her to go to the office she quips, "Teacher's always pickin' on girls." How Miguel and María choose the language to enact their roles is closely associated with their individual perception of the role. Creative elaboration is seen to the extent that they integrate meaningful social expressions into a dialogue which is primarily a direct imitation of the teacher and student role models.

Children use creative elaboration to further develop their perception of the model's role. Language learned through social interactions is added to carbon-copy imitations to supply the missing details of the dialogue and to enliven the conversation. As children develop proficiency in the second language, creative elaborations are noted more frequently than direct imitations of role models. Children combine and transform words in addition to using stylized phrases and social expressions to role-play intense dramatic scenarios.

Finally, children learn English as a second language through social imitation. From this standpoint, the Copycatting strategy facilitates linguistic expression as children try out, adapt, and develop language in a social context, mimic the language of social role models, engage in social problem solving, and practice the social functions of language.

A unique feature of role-playing is that it develops language through social interactions. Martlew et al. (1978) did a study to explore the relationship of language use and speech adaptation to role and social context. Findings of this study suggest that role-play has an important function in the development of children's ability to communicate effectively. Communication in role-play obliges students not only to imitate language patterns but to structure these patterns in accordance with the role-play's theme. Imitated phrases must also be spontaneously adapted to the responses of role-play partners. María, taking the role of the teacher, adapted her mimicked instructional phrases to Miguel's correct or incorrect responses. Miguel's imitation of the teacher's disciplinary expressions was an adaptation to the role María assumed as unruly student. Adapting language to responses of role-play partners in varied social contexts eventually enables children to restructure imitated phrases into creative expression in English.

Creative expression results from an intimate understanding of English syntactical structure and word meaning. Cole (1976) reports that children learn word meaning better when they are embedded in a game of role-play rather than taught as isolated units. Children practice vocabulary in a holistic manner as the words flow from the role-play's action. Ching (1969) did a study of English as a second-language training and found role-play gave children the best practice in the correct use of words and social idioms. Another study by Leonard (1975) reported that children acquired syntactical structures more readily when they were exposed to role-play. The strategy of learning a second language through role-playing thus not only encourages linguistic adaptation but is an impetus to vocabulary building, correct syntax usage in English and finally creative expression.

Central to children's learning sociolinguistic behavior in English is the enactment of social roles. Social roles are organizations of functionally interdependent relationships (Peretti 1977). Some interdependent relationships are mother-child, teacher-student, friend-friend, and salesperson-customer. Roles are functionally interdependent in that linguistic characterization of one half of each dyad is based on the responses of the partner. Characterization of the social role of teacher thus depends on the responses of the partner who enacts the part of student.

Radically different language is needed for varied social role relationships. During role-play, children "imitate images" in social relationships. In this way they experiment with diverse aspects of interpersonal language. Dramatizing a mother-child dyad, the child taking the mother's role mimics informal language usage, stressing terms of endearment such as "sweetie," "honey," and "cutie." If the partner role-plays a naughty child, the mother's language takes on a more negative tone. Role-playing a teacher instructing a student requires more complex utterances, issuing commands, and asking questions. Friend-to-friend dialogue calls for collaborative linguistic patterns including social peer group expressions.

Children develop social scripts initially around people with whom they have a relationship. Labov (1966) states that children pick their models according to strong positive or negative valences. Children choose to copycat those people around them with whom they can identify in some way. Role-play is later extended from identification with specific individuals to generalized types, such as: police, salespersons, doctors, detectives, and astronauts. Language of these social role models is imitated as children invent relationships and develop characterizations as part of the sociodrama. By copycatting social roles, children imitate the language styles of many different participants in the classroom as well as in the outside world. Second language is learned holistically as thought units are integrated into the identity of the social role.

Language must be tailored to fit individual social interactions. Hymes (1974) states, ". . . along with acquiring a system of grammar, children also acquire a social system of use regarding persons, places and other modes of communication. . . . in such acquisition resides children's sociolinguistic competence." Children develop sociolinguistic competence in the second language as they learn to adapt their speech to listeners in different social situations.

Through social role-play, children learn to be skillful in expressing themselves differentially talking to the principal or to a peer. Children imitate the language they have heard English speakers use with the principal as they reenact a school scenario. They mimic the expressions used by TV characters in different social settings. In this way, during role-play, children practice appropriate English expressions and learn to modify their speech for effective conversational interchanges.

Social problem solving during role-play assists children in developing language for evaluation. Children mimic the language of the teacher as arbitrator to gain a sense of how language can be used for social manipulation or for the creation of group solidarity. The second culture's values are also explored during social problem solving in role-play. This is especially important where values differ between cultures. In copycatting role models, children attempt to find some viable personal reconciliation to cultural patterns, values, and attitudes intersecting roles.

The imitation of a range of alternative social roles develops the social functions of language in English. Role-play allows children to practice the functions of language meaningfully in diverse social situations. Halliday (1973) has identified functions of language universally used to communicate meaning to others. These are:

1. Instrumental language — "I want" or "I need." Language is used to satisfy needs or desires. Very often it takes the form of a request.

2. Regulatory language — "Do this" or "Stop it!" Language is used to control the behavior of other people.

3. Interactional language — "Let's play" or "You and me." The speaker uses language to establish and define social relationships and to participate in the "give and take" of social intercourse.

4. Personal language — "Here I am!" Language is used to express one's individuality or to give personal opinions and feelings.

5. Imaginative language — "Let's pretend." The speaker uses language to express fantasies or to create an imaginary world.

6. Heuristic language — "I wonder why?" The speaker uses language to find out about things, to ask questions, to seek information.

7. Informative language — "I've got something to tell you." Language is used by a speaker to give information about the world he or she has experienced.

The functions of language are the building blocks for constructing a linguistic repertoire in the second language. Halliday (1973) notes that it is important for children to have experience with many kinds of talk. Role-playing gives students the opportunity to try out the whole range of language functions. It also gives them practice in tailoring language functions to fit the social context.

Children copycat dominantly instrumental or task-oriented roles as they "play store." The child who plays the customer must ask the shopkeeper for what he wants: "I want cornflakes." The heuristic function is also developed during this role-play theme. The shopkeeper asks the customer what he wants to purchase. The customer asks questions to find out how much things cost or to discover where an item may be located. As they assume the roles of shopkeeper and customer, children imitate the language they have heard in stores around them.

Language used to control the behavior of others, the regulatory function, is practiced by enacting the teacher's role. Copycatting the teacher's language, Miguel and María express many regulatory statements, such as: "Sit down! Pick up the paper!"; "You gonna stay after!"; "I want you right down the office—right now!"

The use of personal language is developed in many role-play settings. Miguel delivers a personal message to María as he says, "I'm very mad at you." Language used to express feelings is often seen in personal messages. Role-playing a domestic theme allows children to imitate the personal language which is part of family interactions.

Interactional language is communicated in role-play improvisations that relate to social problem solving. Children role-play how it feels to be left out or what a friend can do to help. They imitate social expressions to relate empathically to others: "You feel bad," "I'm sorry," "What's the matter?" In this way children practice the language necessary for establishing interpersonal relationships with English speakers.

Children practice informative language use in any role-play theme that calls for the actors to give information. Explanatory statements are part of the informative function. Miguel and María use this type of language as they explain the math lesson: "Count seven, now two, now three"; "Now put up three more." As the children explain the math lesson, they are also developing the informative function of language. Role-playing a travel agent allows children to practice giving the tourist information about a particular location or directions for how to get somewhere.

The imaginative linguistic function is integrated as children portray those roles which consist of elements that do not relate to their own experience. Children can role-play a doctor, a police officer, or an astronaut without having experienced all aspects of the role. The doctor's role may not be known beyond shot-giving. Children thus imitate the role model from their experience and use their imagination to creatively elaborate the missing details.

Expanding the full range of language functions through role-play permits children to learn the second language through social imitation and creative elaboration in meaningful communicative situations. Role-play creates a range of situations in which students may practice a variety of social functions in English. The end goal of role-play is to prepare students to effectively function in the English speech community.

By affectively, selectively, creatively, individually, and socially imitating role models, children learn English as a second language. The strategy of Copycatting permits children to practice English words and phrases by imitating images with definite social scripts. Affect is developed as children gain an intuitive understanding of the second language through style of voice and the matching of words to nonverbal behaviors. English expressions are expanded as children must adapt their responses to their partner during role-play. Children also learn to tailor English responses to match specific social situations.

Role-play encourages the spontaneous use of imitated language in lifelike situations. Creative elaboration in role-play conversations leads to unique styles of expression in the second language. Linguistic flexibility and cultural understanding is reinforced through role-playing a collection of social roles. Ultimately, the strategy of Copycatting enables children to integrate English expression into a complete system of communication and cultural identification.

IMPLICATIONS OF COPYCATTING
FOR SECOND-LANGUAGE LEARNING
AND CLASSROOM TEACHING

Social role-play is an important classroom technique for developing conversational competency in the second language. Role-play facilitates affective expression and provides the impetus for children to try out social roles. Dramatic dialogues can be encouraged in the classroom both as free imaginative play and through structured activities.

Free imaginative role-play is stimulated by the teacher who arranges a "special place" in the classroom for creative expression. This section of the room should include blocks, puppets, props, and clothing for role-play. Props can be divided into boxes by theme such as: the school box, the hospital box, the airport box, and the farm box. Children can then freely choose a box and utilize the props to create a dramatic improvisation. Blocks can be built into a bus, a store or a sailboat with children taking on the roles of bus driver, shopkeeper or sailor. Thematic role-play boxes can be changed weekly or seasonally. Other ideas for props for older children include: historical boxes, international boxes, and old-time costume boxes.

Structured role-play activities can be devised by the teacher to capture students' interest. Stories, fables, movies, and filmstrips can provide the stimulus for children to reenact characters' roles. Another variation of this idea is to have students make puppets of their favorite character with a partner. A game called "Changing Partners" can be played. Every five to ten minutes partners and puppets are exchanged and children role-play with a new partner. This activity provides a lot of language practice.

Pairing students for story-telling also provides second-language practice opportunities. The teacher can set the stage by telling the class a story about a definite theme, such as the most frightening thing that ever happened to him or her. After the teacher's rendition of the story, children are divided into pairs and asked to tell each other the most frightening thing that has happened to them. Children are then asked to role-play each others' stories for the class.

Older children who are reading can be assigned roles to play that are designated on 3 × 5 cards. The cards describe the position of each character and may supply two or three lines of dialogue. The teacher sets up the role-play situation by describing the event depicted by the dialogue. Student-pairs then act out the event using the language provided on the card, as well as ad-libbing with additional imitated English phrases.

Role-play may also be structured around TV programs and telephone conversations. Students can be given the opportunity to dramatize social situations from TV scenes. Children can practice social and personal functional language usage by carrying on a good telephone conversation. Gossip situations provide good "situational set-ups" for role play. Older students especially like to communicate about themes such as: a new boy or girl at school, the party, the vacation, lost papers or an invitation to the movies.

Interviewing is a powerful technique for role-play. The teacher or students can pretend to be some well-known personality or imaginative figure. Their partner "plays" a reporter and interviews him or her. One teacher employed the interviewing method by taking the role of a lady from Zanzibar with twenty-two children. The teacher set the stage by telling the children that they were newspaper reporters on assignment to interview the "Mother of the Year." One child gave the following introduction to the class:

> Ladies and gentlemen of the press, may I present Madame Mbuter of Zanzibar, mother of twenty-two children, who has come to the United States to accept the "Mother of the Year" award. Please take turns interviewing her (Berkowitz 1972).

Children in the class took turns asking questions relating to how it felt to care for twenty-two offspring.

This interviewing technique can be built upon by having children interview community and school personnel, such as the principal or nurse. Tape recordings of interviews permit the class to listen to other children's interviews and provides the opportunity for the teacher to give feedback. Through the interviewing technique, students practice formulating questions in the second language.

Questioning and information-giving are two important social functions of language. These functions can be integrated into sociodrama role-playing activities. One popular sociodrama is a courtroom case where children take the parts of witnesses and lawyers. The teacher may play the role of the judge and ask children (playing lawyers), to rephrase questions. Witnesses can be asked to elaborate on descriptions. The teacher should take the following steps in setting up the sociodrama:

1. explain the situation to the class
2. select the case
3. role-play situation
4. talk about role-play
5. select a new cast and do it again

By reenacting a scene children have the opportunity to see roles played in a different way. They are also exposed to various patterns of English language responses.

Role-playing for problem solving develops language around students' interests, cares, internal feelings, and attitudes. A problem solving role-play session consists of a situation involving two or more people in which some action must be taken to correct a difficult situation. The sequences of activities involves: delineating a situation, proposing a course of action, presenting new vocabulary, conducting an enactment, and discussing the solutions (Shaftel 1970). Social problems that can be role-played are: how it feels to be left out of a game, being called names, and feelings about having to move to another state and leaving friends. A social theme can be introduced by the teacher in the following manner: "People have different ways to solve problems. Role-play with a friend how you'd solve this one." The teacher further builds on affective language use by asking, "How does it feel to be in this situation?" Role-playing emotional situations gives insight into people's diverse solutions to social problems. It also expands alternative English language expressions. Students may have very strong feelings about some of these situations, thus ample opportunities for discussion are presented.

Comedy routines are a very enjoyable way for children to learn the second language. These routines can be based on affective imitation and repetition of language patterns. An example of a comedy routine which teaches the pattern of "on the table" is about a "smart aleck" telling someone exactly where to put a book. The teacher instructs students by modeling the dialogue and having them chorally respond. Then children are asked to take turns acting out the comedy routine. The teacher should encourage children to be very funny as they enact the part of the smart aleck. The comedy routine is as follows:

Child: Put it on the table.

Smart Aleck: On the table. . . . Don't you want it on the desk?
             (Puts book on the desk)

Child:	Put it on the table.
Smart Aleck:	On the table. . . . Don't you want it on your head? (Puts book on child's head)
Child:	Put it on the table.
Smart Aleck:	On the table. . . . Don't you want it on the floor? (Puts book on the floor) etc.

Comedy cross-talk, such as this dialogue, provides natural repetition of English verbal patterns in the context of a role-play scenario.

Pantomimic activities accompanied by dialogue can also be used to develop the imaginative function of language. Brief pantomimed sketches teach vocabulary through characterization. The teacher can instruct the children to pantomime various inanimate objects and then have the rest of the class describe what it feels like to be that particular object. For example, a student can pantomime a washing machine, an ice-cream cone or a statue and then the teacher can generate a lively discussion about the child's actions. Children may also enjoy role-playing specific situations about such characters as: a scared mountain climber, a cook who burns everything, a pirate searching for treasure or a fire fighter saving people in a burning building. Students can exaggerate their motions in order to convey the appropriate emotions. Through pantomime activities like these, children can imitate behavior while using imaginative language to project ideas and feelings.

Children can also role-play different human reactions and emotions by playing a game called "Changing Hats." The teacher can supply a box full of various hats such as a baby bonnet, a woman's flowery and feathery hat, a baseball cap and a man's hat. Have children pick out a hat and put it on. Then have them tell the other children about a particular incident (vacation, party, trip) using the appropriate language as implied by the hat they chose. Discuss how their vocabulary changed and why.

Other role-play games are:

Occupation Game: Each student is given a picture of a person doing something that relates to his or her occupation. The teacher initiates the lesson by giving some basic information about different occupations. Students act out the role of the person engaged in an occupational action using words and gestures. Children have to guess the person's occupation.

People-Maker: One child takes the part of the people-maker, someone who operates a factory that makes people. All of the people are made on an imaginary belt. The people-maker asks each child how he or she wants to be made. Responses such as "I'd like to be made with my ears on my hands so I could put my hands in my pockets and keep my ears warm" or "I'd like to have my feet on my head so that I could walk upside-down" can be generated in this way.

Looking Out: Children role-play the parts of animals or fish looking out of a cage or fish tank. Empathetic personal language is developed as children describe what it's like to be looked at all day.

<u>Magic Potion</u>: One child has magic potions. He or she role-plays with a partner the changes that are brought about through the use of the potion. The partner is made smaller, fatter or taller and most role-play his or her feelings about these changes.

Role-play encourages affective language expression. Students not only imitate language during role-play but use their faces, hands, and body to display emotions like sadness, glee, love or fear. Enacting a theme allows language to evolve naturally rather than mechanically and creates a meaningful situation to practice the second language. The teacher plays a multidimensional role in staging social scenarios by becoming costume coordinator, script manager, prompter, and director. As dramas evolve, teachers can enjoy a scope of unlimited creativity in the classroom world of "Show-Biz" as children role-play in the second language.

On the Map

The teacher has presented a lesson on people around the world. She made use of the globe to point out the continents, alluding to them by color. She then assigned tasks to small groups of students. One group is making an African village. Another group is dressing some paper dolls in regional costumes. Miguel and María are assigned the task of putting together a map of the world. The teacher gives the children the following directions:

Teacher: Van a hacer este rompecabezas dentro del marco para formar el mapa del mundo. You are going to put the pieces on this puzzle. Estos pedazos forman los países y los continentes del mundo. Son de colores diferentes. Fíjense bien en los colores. Pongan los pedazos aquí en el mapa. Put the pieces on the map. See, put the red pieces on the map. Put the ocean on the map. Put the blue pieces on the map. Put Africa on the map.

(You are going to put together this puzzle inside the frame to make up a map of the world. These pieces make up the countries and the continents of the world. They are different colors. Pay attention to the colors. Put the pieces here on the map.)

Miguel: Vamos a poner estos pedazos—en el mapa, on the map, on the map.
(Let's put these pieces on the map.)

María: (Looks carefully at a puzzle piece, studying its shape and noting its color.)
Aquí está blue.
(Here is blue.)

Miguel: Put blue on the map.

María: Sí, blue.

Miguel: (Takes various pieces and sets about putting them together. He gets the globe and looks for patterns. He then arranges the pieces together in corresponding configurations. He takes a group of red pieces and joins them.)
The red on the map.

María: (Taking Miguel's joined pieces off the puzzle frame)
No, no, solamente uno red. (No, no, only one red.)

Miguel: No, estos pedazos se pueden poner todos juntos on the map.
            (No, you can put all these pieces together on the map.)

María: No, no juntos, uno después del otro.
            (No, not together, one after the other.)
            Put red here. Put red here.
            (María puts one red piece at a time on the puzzle frame.)

Miguel: (Putting in several pieces)
            All red, blue, white on the map.

LANGUAGE STYLE STRATEGY
AND SECOND-LANGUAGE LEARNING
PUTTING IT TOGETHER

Miguel and María are presented with an empty puzzle frame and a myriad of pieces. Their task is to organize the pieces to fit into the frame, thus forming a map of the world. Each child becomes a Sherlock Holmes in search of clues in his or her attempt to put together the pieces in order to see the total picture. While the end result for both children is that of integration of the parts into a whole, Miguel and María each manifest a distinct predisposition as to how the process of placing the pieces in the frame should be structured. Miguel looks for spatial configurations on the globe and arranges several pieces on the frame in corresponding patterns. María, on the other hand, insists that pieces be integrated one at a time in a unitary fashion. The *modus operandi* each child chooses to approach this task has some regular and predictable characteristics, such as attending to patterns versus individual parts, from which a problem solving style can be inferred. Just as children manifest different styles of approach for integrating pieces in the puzzle frame, they also reveal distinct styles of framing their second-language learning. Language learning corresponds to solving a puzzle. The learning of the second language presents children with a unique verbal problem. Children must unravel the meaning of words and phrases and fit them into a total linguistic system. To do this, children adopt a strategy to frame their initial language learning. Second-language learning may thus be thought of as a framing process.

How children think, their cognitive style, frames how they begin to learn language. This framing process is encompassed in the **Putting It Together** strategy. This strategy attempts to bridge cognitive, motivational, and social predispositions into characteristic styles of second-language learning. It emphasizes that children vary significantly in their initial language organization and that such variation in style affects cognitive and linguistic processes in learning the second language. Among the strategies children bring to bear is an organizing hypothesis as to how language is to be learned. Each child chooses to magnify one of several salient characteristics of language: phonology—the sounds of language; semantics—word meaning; or syntax—pattern or structure of words in a phrase or sentence. Children then use one of these features to structure and frame what they attend to in language acquisition. Language learning style, characterized by the Putting It Together strategy, is thus defined as an initially consistent predisposition to structure language learning in a particular way. Style defines not only how learners process linguistic information but clearly manifests what aspect of language they choose to focus their attention on to derive meaning. Style sets the frame for language production. It also accounts for the fact that children learn language by differing routes. Lynch (1961) talks about "wayfinding as the original function of environmental structuring." Style acts as a map for the initial direction of second-language learning and serves as a frame of reference within which children can gain knowledge of a new linguistic system. Style is like the puzzle frame in that it gives children the foundation onto which they can construct and fit pieces of linguistic information. Style is a special tool, a complex cognitive structure for framing language learning.

Children's strategic use of language interacts with their cognitive organization of the world. The learning of language and the development of cognition have certain intellectual processes in common. The search for commonalities in sorting out the multitude of sense impressions that impinge upon children is one of the shared features of language and cognition. Cohen (1969) refers to the process by which children organize, classify, and assimilate linguistic information as "integrated rule sets for the selection and organization of sense and linguistic data." Children are thus seen as active processors of language. Children learn language through linguistic interactions. In these interactions children attend selectively to certain features of language. They store words in memory according to the stylistic approach taken. They may store words by phonetic features, or by patterns determined by semantics or by syntax.

Three styles of language learning can be identified. They correspond to the three elements of language and can be distinguished by observing children's behavior in second-language learning. The production of language is an overt process and its acquisition, therefore, should be thought of in terms of overt practice. The way children choose to practice a language, then, is one way of determining their approach to the language learning task.

The three styles of language learning manifested in children's conversations and other linguistic interactions are labeled Beading, Braiding, and Orchestrating. Each one of these styles frames the language learning process for individual children and allows them to integrate linguistic information into a total system of meaning as well as providing the structure for language production.

Styles of language learning are characterized by a "feature learning theory" as proposed by Olson (1970). The essential differences in the three styles lie in the encoding and performance requirements. Each language style is built on the coding of different features of language. The child who is oriented toward looking for patterns of language (syntax) will encode very different aspects of the language learning environment from the one who is oriented to encoding sounds (phonology). The production of language will also correspond to the aspect of language on which the child focuses.

María's use of language in the dialogue manifests the **Beading** style of language learning. María concentrates on the meaning of individual words (semantics). She carefully studies the color of each puzzle piece and then bridges the English color word to label it. María places the pieces on the puzzle frame one at a time. She is extremely uncomfortable when Miguel wants to put a number of pieces together for placement on the puzzle frame. She tells him, "No, no juntos, uno después del otro." (No, not together, one after the other.) María's problem solving approach is to go from individual parts to the whole. This approach corresponds to her language learning style. María learns words as discrete elements. She relates words to concrete objects at first, such as the color word "blue" to the blue puzzle part. She later classifies words and organizes them by their semantic features. María frames her second-language learning around understanding individual word meaning in context.

In a classroom, Beaders can be identified as the children who respond more to one-word utterances. They begin the language learning process by generating names for objects. They interpret the language learning task as calling for object identification rather than description. They attend to meaning of individual words and isolate those features of the context which give words their maximum intelligibility. Beaders perceive words as separate entities requiring differentiation from other elements. Thus, words of sentences are considered as separate parts whose meaning is understood in isolation rather than as an integral part of a complete thought. Beaders respond selectively to particular words that directly name or describe individual elements in the environment. Fillmore (1976) describes the response of a child named Juan to an elicitation task in which he was asked to describe a picture. His response is typical of the Beader's approach:

> Juan used only words he knew well. He resorted to his tactics of naming and accounting for all the participants in the picture and doing no more. Juan isolated those aspects of the picture he could name and didn't attend to the rest of the picture.

Juan was concerned with meaning of individual words. He utilized the Beading approach to second-language learning in this example by framing his response around naming individual elements and disregarding the total action that the picture revealed.

Beaders can be described as incremental learners. These students learn language as a gradual process. They are learners whose style is to undertake one problem at a time and to work it out completely before going on to the next. They proceed to learn the second language in a step-by-step fashion, systematically adding bits and pieces together to gain a larger understanding of the new linguistic system. The beading analogy which illustrates this language learning style refers to the careful and tedious process of adding bead upon bead to develop the larger structure of a necklace (language system). Each word is learned as a segment to be added individually in a process that will ultimately result in learning a total linguistic system.

Beaders demonstrate an analytic or inductive problem solving style.

Analysis involves learning words on the basis of distinguishing features and emphasizes concepts and contextual meaning. Beaders differentiate words by small concept domains such as food or animals. They appear to set about learning the second language as a cognitive code by sorting, analyzing, and classifying the words they hear. They abstract individual elements from sentences and string them together as content words. Beaders are children who from the beginning of the language learning process have little difficulty learning and using words that name people and objects. They learn words best in isolated contexts where they can make a direct association of an object with the oral production of its label. They also learn words easily by associated pairs of native language and English equivalent words in context. By learning individual words in context they develop a concept knowledge of the meanings embodied in words. Beaders concentrate on nouns. Verbs are more difficult for them. They have difficulty in recalling appropriate words for describing activities even when the verbs are modeled by the teacher or peers. Children who reveal the beading style tend to adopt all-purpose verbs. They treat the language learning task as if their chief goal is to ferret out objects to identify. Beaders manifest a singularity of approach to second-language learning. They appear to need to get the nouns under control before learning verbs. Their productive use of language is thus based on naming objects. Object names are added as stationary beads on the string. Words do not change places or interact because the action words on which the language moves are missing from the initial language-acquisition process adopted by Beaders.

The Beading style can be described as a horizontal process of language learning. Children who utilize this style as a strategy for "putting language together" connect words in a linear manner. Words may be thought of as disenfranchised parts of a puzzle. Beaders deal with isolated parts of language. Little attention is given to patterns or relationships. Words are strung one after another. They are added in one direction and based on only one aspect of language word meaning (semantics). Attention is focused on the content of language rather than form.

Children who tend to learn language by the Beading style consistently place a strong emphasis on the comprehension of language initially. They usually produce a limited number of words in the early stages of second-language learning. They rely on the internal processing of language they hear in advance of their linguistic production. The Beading style can be labeled as conservative. Children who have this language learning style don't want to use a word until they fully comprehend it. They thus carefully control the number of words encoded. Words are knotted together carefully in this bead-necklace analogy. Therefore, each bead added to the necklace is clearly understood and produced before the knot is tied after the bead, making it an integral part of the necklace.

In summary, the Beading style describes children who are incremental learners. They learn and encode words by meaning (semantics) usually defined in context. They produce language only when they gain a receptive understanding of the meaning of words. Their initial language production will be to label objects, identifying nouns before they learn verbs. Beaders frame the second language around individual word meaning.

In contrast to the Beading style, Miguel approaches language learning from a completely different perspective. This is revealed initially in his strategy of putting together the puzzle. He immediately takes several pieces of the puzzle and starts joining them. He searches for configurations of continents on the globe and then interlinks puzzle pieces to match the patterns. While María asserts her desire for a piece-by-piece approach to puzzle completion, Miguel seems predisposed to tying more than one piece together in an integrated manner where relationships between pieces is of primary importance. He responds to María's insistence that pieces must be put on the puzzle frame in a unitary fashion by saying, "No estos pedazos se pueden poner todos juntos on the map." (No, you can put all these pieces together on the map.)

The integrative, generalizing strategy Miguel uses for solving the puzzle is carried over to his language learning style. Miguel frames the second-language learning process around form (syntax). He looks for patterns in the way language is structured. He attends to the sequential arrangement of words or chunks, analogous to phrases in language. Miguel searches for commonalities in sorting out a multitude of linguistic expressions. He acquires the second language in chunks. He does this by gathering chunks or phrases from various contexts and then practicing them in social interactions.

Miguel quickly assimilates the phrase "on the map." He derives meaning initially from the teacher's code switching in the context of the direction giving. He tests his understanding of the phrase as he compares the English phrase "on the map" to its Spanish translation, "en el mapa." Miguel contrasts and repeats the phrases "en el mapa, on the map, on the map." He then generalizes the phrase by making a series of statements about the puzzle pieces.

Put blue *on the map*.
The red *on the map*.
No estos pedazos se pueden poner todos juntos *on the map*.
All red, blue, white *on the map*.

Miguel thus practices the language chunk "on the map" as a new structure in a meaningful context. By manipulating chunks as holistic structures, Miguel eventually masters the formal features of the syntax of the English language.

The language learning style Miguel applies to the process of second-language acquisition is termed **Braiding.** The Braiding style differs significantly from the Beading approach. While Beaders were noted to acquire language by learning individual words as isolated elements of meaning, Braiders internalize language on the level of language patterns or chunks. The analogy of braiding to describe this learning style depicts how individual strands (words) are chunked together (phrases) and then the chunks combined by crossing one over the other (Braiding). Where chunks cross, patterns are common. This means that chunks like "on the map" are used over and over in various contexts until they are learned. In this language style, children learn the second language by concentrating on phrases and weaving them as patterns into the braid, which will eventually be tied at the bottom, denoting a completed linguistic system.

In the classroom, Braiders are those children who begin immediately to use social phrases and chunks of language in context. Little analysis is called for. Children have only to attend to what context and under what circumstances an expression is uttered. Braiders figure out phrases and the roles they play in sentences by functions and relationships. As certain chunks turn up in many linguistic interactions, these patterns become an ordering element on which children can base future language production. The capability of expressing thoughts by relating one phrase to the next gradually increases as language ability develops. The learning of a series of patterns reduces the complexity of the linguistic system and facilitates oral production of the second language.

The Braiding style depends on imitation and substitution of modeled patterns. Children relying on this language learning style can very early produce sentences with a minimum of effort. Braiders use chunks as frames to formulate sentences mechanically. They make gradual adjustments so that the patterns become flexible enough to be used in a number of language productions. A number of versions of sentences can be based on chunks by following the word order of modeled sentences. This is clearly illustrated in the number of sentences Miguel produced with the chunk "on the map."

Braiders, unlike Beaders, who dwell on receptive understanding of individual word meaning, put their emphasis on the oral production of language. Meaning is generated for Braiders in dynamic patterns. Form is paid attention to as a tactic to abstract usable chunks of language. Braiders learn chunks and then try them out in social interactions, thus bringing their newly acquired competence into use.

Jesus, a boy in Fillmore's study (1976), manifests the Braider style as he describes a picture:

Boy, play little ball.
Girl, play little ball.
Two boys, play little ball.
Two girls, play little ball.

Jesus uses the same chunk (play little ball) to create several sentences. The meaning of the chunk is reinforced through the use of the phrase in context.

For children who adopt the Braiding style, the most parsimonious way of learning language is to learn it in patterns and allow meaning to emerge through usage.

Whereas Beaders were said to manifest an analytical language learning style, Braiders reveal a relational approach to second-language learning. Relational style is defined by Cohen (1969):

> The relational style of learning requires a descriptive mode of abstraction. . . . only the global characteristics of a stimulus have meaning to its users, and those only in reference to some total context.

Braiders master the second language relationally and deductively. They proceed from the general informal use of language patterns to later breaking down patterns to create new word arrangements. Braiders pay attention to form and the sequence of words rather than to individual word meaning. This is in direct contrast to the Beading style, which is a formal, analytic, inductive mode of acquiring language where words are segmented as units of meaning.

The Braiding style can be thought of as a vertical process rather than the horizontal procedure which denoted the Beading model. Braiders use a spiraling linkage of patterns. In the braid, the chunks are crossed at many junctures. They are coterminous. This process illustrates how patterns of language are joined at many points as they are intertwined to invent a network of language. Braiders demonstrate a fluid system of language production which depends greatly on collaboration with native speakers, who are both the models and reinforcers of their attempts to practice the syntax of the second language in meaningful contexts.

The Braiding style can be summarized as a relational, deductive, and collaborative language learning style. Braiders frame their second-language acquisition around patterns of language they learn through interactions with native speakers. Children with this style concentrate initially on form (syntax), the way patterns are structured rather than individual word meaning. They derive meaning through the use of language sequences in social contexts. The Braiding style is a vertical process where patterns of language are overlapped and woven together as they are integrated into a braid or complete linguistic system.

Quite distinct from Beading and Braiding is a third style of language learning called **Orchestrating.** Orchestrators are children who are preoccupied with the sounds of the second language (phonology) and place initial emphasis on listening comprehension. Processing of auditory input is essential and intrinsic to this method of framing language. Orchestrators are concerned with the accurate reproduction of sounds. They do not treat these sounds in isolation but orchestrate them into the resonant sound patterns which distinguish the English language.

In the classroom these children attend carefully to intonations and rhythms that characterize English speech patterns. They understand what is said by tone of speech. Context is less important. Children focus on developing a feeling for phonological cues which enhance language intelligibility, trying to absorb sound patterns of the linguistic code before they begin to speak.

Orchestrators tune in to the second language much as one tunes in to a radio, trying to adjust the sound volume so one can make sense of the song. The second language is learned like a melody which is rhythmically controlled. Orchestrators tune in to all the vibrations of sound that are part of the second-language speaking environment. The everyday routines of speech become many varied rhythmic patterns for Orchestrators. Phonetic models are synchronized into speech productions. Orchestrators emphasize the accurate elicitation of rhythmic patterns and intonations because of the intimate relationship of these sound patterns with syntax. The sounds of the second language are related to the context of available redundant cues of syntax. Children abstract the sound distinctions from syntax.

Orchestrators can also be classified as phonetic imitators. They are quite dependent on language models. They are guided by the rhythm of the sentence prototypes. Unless a sentence is carefully modeled, Orchestrators cannot reproduce it. Because meaning isn't a feature of this initial second-language learning method, Orchestrators must depend on their immediate short-term memory to recall and parrot what is spoken. Therefore, Orchestrators are usually only able to reproduce parts of what they've heard. They emit sentence segments with little or no understanding of what they are saying. Sentence segments generated may vary significantly from the order of modeled sentences.

Orchestrators concentrate on intonation following the first-language acquisition process. Jolly (1975) speaks of "interactional synchrony" to characterize the way first language is learned. This term describes babies' innate responsiveness to the rhythm of speech patterns and word intonations. Orchestrators rely on intonations and differences in phonological elements to facilitate language learning and to make sense of the sounds of the new linguistic system. Orchestrators first put together meaningless sequences of sounds. Later, these sounds are orchestrated into words and sentences.

As children conduct the process of orchestrating sounds into words, they become aware of how sound units are segmented into syllables and how these syllables in turn make up words. Orchestrators usually deal with the sounds of beginning and ending words and phrases. They tend to verbalize noun phrases which usually occur at the beginning and ending of sentences. They lose the middle of sentences as part of the memory recall process which states, as part of learning theory, that the middle of a verbalized task is harder to remember. They therefore produce sentences without verbs. Fillmore (1976) notes that children who demonstrate this style omit verbs to preserve the rhythmic contour of utterances. They mumble uninterruptively between noun phrases.

She describes these children as inventing verb-like forms or mock verbs. Children insert these nonsense forms indiscriminately as "placeholders" to take the place of verbs they cannot remember and to preserve the rhythmic flow of language.

The third style of language learning can be seen in totality as a mode of second-language acquisition that is framed almost entirely on auditory input. Children's learning is dependent on their ability to discriminate and pronounce sounds. Later, they must attend to the rules that govern how sounds are combined into words and larger units. Children with this style see the task of second-language learning as orchestrating a series of sounds from memory, relying on native speakers as models. They orchestrate sounds first by syllables, then words, then as sentences to compose a symphony or a completed composition of the second language.

An evaluation of these styles leads one to conclude that children undertake to learn a second language in several different ways. Second-language learners face the task of grasping, distinguishing, and retaining an enormous variety of linguistic forms. Children, in order not to become overwhelmed by this formidable task, develop an approach, a preferred technique, a language learning style to frame language acquisition.

Language learning style frames second-language acquisition in that it defines the element of the language code that is attended to by children. It structures the way children react and adapt to the linguistic environment and attack the second language. Language style is a dynamic building process in which children are architects who instinctively formulate a hypothetical model for second-language learning. The framework for the model is based on individual children's predisposition or style which serves to tie together linguistic elements. Having an established framework, children go into the lumberyard (classroom) and search for those pieces of wood (elements of language) that fit their framework and allow them to build and put together the second language.

Beading, Braiding, and Orchestrating are language learning frames that enable children to apply the Putting It Together strategy. The Beading style frames language in terms of word meaning (semantics). Here the learning of vocabulary is the basic element used in language building. The process of construction proceeds in a linear additive set in which each piece of wood (word) is selected and added individually. The Braiding style is framed around language patterns (syntax). Attention is paid not to individual pieces of wood but to the arrangement of the wood in patterns in order to erect a latticework for second-language learning. The style of Orchestrating frames language around auditory input (phonology). Concentration is on the sounds that are part of the building process.

No one style is the best way to learn language, and styles are not always mutually exclusive. Some styles are more efficacious than others in allowing children to initially produce language, such as the Braiding style. The advantage of Braiders in initially more active production is, however, for the most part equalized by users of the other styles as children become more immersed in the English linguistic system, when all of the three styles may be combined later in a holistic process of learning.

Language learning style is an important concept because it addresses the fact that children at first frame second-language learning in different terms and in different forms. Styles delineate how children process language, what they pay attention to, and the content of what they initially learn.

IMPLICATIONS OF PUTTING IT TOGETHER FOR SECOND-LANGUAGE LEARNING AND CLASSROOM TEACHING

Teachers can facilitate the second-language learning process for children by building on learning styles with the classroom methodology. Teachers can do this by understanding four key elements of second-language instruction. The first key feature is to provide children with opportunities to use language across subject areas, paying attention to tailoring input around learning styles. Second, it is important to be aware that language is a social-expressive tool. This means that the context in which learning takes place is very important for facilitating language use for real communicative purposes. Children with different learning styles should have opportunities to interact on meaningful social or cognitive tasks. The teacher gets this interaction to take place by providing for different participant structures, or ways of arranging verbal interactions with students for communicating different types of educational material and for providing variation in social interactions that take place in the classroom. One participant structure would be to interact with the whole class. Another would be to interact with groups of a given style. Formal and informal groups also differently structure the language learning experience. Differences in students' readiness to participate in interactions is related to the way the interaction is originated and controlled so that the child feels comfortable using the second language. Thirdly, language instruction directed at each style should address three domains of language—cognitive, affective, and social—to give children linguistic flexibility.

Finally, the teacher should seek to individualize ESL instruction. The degree to which children's dominant ways of framing language match the teacher's instructional method is the issue here. Individualization is defined by Henry (1975) as "an attitude of teaching students as individual persons." The scope of this concept includes goals for each learner, method, and individual pacing of instruction with various degrees of structure.

The extent to which the four instructional elements presented can be incorporated into lesson planning will determine how easily children will learn the second language. Each language learning style is complemented by specific instructional methods and various classroom organizational patterns.

The Beading style is complemented by context-oriented presentation of English words across language domains. The context presentation is important because it allows Beaders to abstract more meaning. Since Beaders frame language learning around meaning, the more meaningful the material to be learned, the greater the facility Beaders will have in learning and retaining what is taught. In addition, the more numerous kinds of associations that are made to an item, the better are learning and retention. Associations of words are made when they are learned in groups or categories such as "clothing," "food," or "animals."

An example of a context-oriented presentation of a lesson on clothing would proceed in the following manner: First, pictures of clothing would be shown by the teacher, and children would be taught English labels (cognitive domain). The visual presentation enables children to derive meaning from the English words by bridging them to their conceptual understanding. The teacher can further tie the clothing labels to a context by asking children to name the clothing they are wearing. The second part of the lesson would be in the affective domain. The teacher would ask children to tell her or him how they feel about what they are wearing or to communicate about how they would feel about wearing one of the articles of clothing labeled in picture cards. The social domain of language would be incorporated into the lesson by involving children in games where group interaction with dominant speakers occurs. Children could be grouped and then given clothing cards for deciding which articles of clothing to take on a trip to various places with different climates. Another game would be to give children sets of cards and have them group clothing cards and sort out cards of other categories. Children learn the social uses of language, including social expressions, as they interact with peers.

Beaders function best in a classroom where lessons have a clearly defined structure. An inductive approach to learning fits their incremental learning style. Beaders become overwhelmed by the presentation of too many concepts at once. The teacher thus must carefully control the number of structures in each lesson so that these children clearly see what they are responsible for learning.

The Braiding style is built upon in the classroom where the teacher encourages social interaction. For Braiders, second-language learning is largely a social undertaking. Braiders learn language across domains as they interact with dominant speakers in large groups, small groups, and in one-to-one interactions. Social interactions allow Braiders to pick up patterns of language and to practice them in social settings, getting reinforcement from native speakers on their uses of English language structures. An ESL lesson for Braiders would proceed as follows: introduce a phrase such as "under the chair" as part of the meaningful pattern practice; hold up pictures and say "the cat is under the chair" (physically placing the cat under the chair); ask children to find and cut out pictures in a magazine of things that can be placed under the chair; have children draw a chair and place objects under it; put children in pairs and ask them to fill each other in on all the things they found which can be placed "under the chair." For example, "The ball is under the chair; the box is under the chair, etc."

Braiders respond well to pattern drills in meaningful contexts. Drills can be structured to include the cognitive, affective, and social domains. Braiders function best in a fairly open-ended classroom environment which fosters exploration.

For Orchestrators, teachers can exploit songs and other rhythmic language compositions as classroom teaching aids. Songs present the communicative aspect of language and the entertainment aspect of music. Songs may be used to teach specific language elements. Songs are particularly effective if presented along with visual aids for receptive understanding of words. Poems with a distinct cadence can be effective also.

Since Orchestrators place so much stress on auditory input and repeating what they hear, teachers should be aware that they are continually serving as models for imitation. Teachers can ease the burden of these children who try to recall exactly what the teacher says by using short sentences and carefully enunciating words. This reduces the load on short term memory for these students. A lesson for Orchestrators would use chants to teach grammatical patterns. A unit on food names would be taught as follows:

Do you like apples? (Teacher holds up picture of apples as children repeat chant.)
Yes, I do.
Do you like grapes?
Yes, I do.

This would be followed by a listening comprehension worksheet. Here children would be given pictures of three fruit in each row: apples, grapes, bananas, etc. The teacher would say: "Do you like bananas?" The children would respond: "Yes, I do." and then would circle the picture of bananas, etc.

The behavior of teachers that reinforces students' language learning styles contributes considerably to the ease in which children learn the second language. The goal of English as a second-language instruction is to allow children to learn English in the way that is suitable to them. For the teacher this requires a sensitivity to the needs of learners as well as a repertoire of instructional methods. The knowledge of language styles should be used as a prerequisite for instructional planning. The teacher's goal should be to provide as many opportunities as possible for children to use language under a wide range of conditions.

In seeing the young language learner as a Beader, Braider or Orchestrator rather than simply as a pupil beginning to learn a second language, the teacher touches upon a new dimension of insight in the instruction process. The learners are uniquely defined and the teaching strategy is effectively developed by Putting It Together.

C'mon Over

The class is enjoying a field trip to a local park. Everyone has brought a sack lunch. The teacher has directed the children to sit together in a circle under a tree while eating their lunches. After lunch the children are given free play. As children gather balls and other play equipment, definite play groups begin to emerge. Many Spanish speakers congregate together, as do the English speakers. Some of the English speakers decide to play baseball. They cross a small bridge and go over to a large grassy area. Bobby (an English speaker) is throwing the ball up and down when he sees Miguel standing with María. He calls to them, "C'mon over and play." The other English speakers echo Bobby, shouting, "C'mon over and play." Miguel grabs a mitt from the play equipment box and tries to convince María to join him and the other children in a game of baseball.

Miguel: María, c'mon and play.

María: No, quiero quedarme aquí con Rosa, Maricela y Carlos.
         (No, I want to stay here with Rosa, Maricela and Carlos.)

Miguel: C'mon, María, I wanna play baseball.

María: Prefiero jugar con mis propios amigos. No quiero jugar con los otros
         niños.
         (I'd rather play with my own friends. I don't want to play with the
         other children.)

Miguel: C'mon, María.

María: No, no sé decir las cosas que quiero en inglés.
(No, I don't know how to say the things I want to in English.)

Miguel: ¡Ven! Yo puedo ayudarte.
(Come! I can help you.)

María: No, quiero quedarme aquí.
(No, I want to stay here.)

Miguel: Entonces, me voy. Here I come! (to English speakers)
(Then, I'm going.)

MOTIVATIONAL STYLE STRATEGY AND SECOND-LANGUAGE LEARNING
CHOOSING THE WAY

"C'mon over and play," shouts Bobby and the other English speakers from across the bridge. On the other side of the bridge are native language Spanish speakers engaged in a game. Miguel and María are faced with the choice of playing with Spanish speakers or crossing over and joining the English speakers. While Miguel chooses to cross over, María is adamant in wanting to remain with her Spanish-speaking friends. Miguel's and María's decisions relate to their motivation to learn the second language by seeking and exploiting practice opportunities. Miguel is motivated to make use of the immediate practice opportunity to interact with English speakers; María is not.

Practice opportunities are defined as all those activities both within and outside the classroom which expose the learner to the English language and which afford him or her the opportunity to practice communicating. Second-language learners are differentially motivated to make use of practice opportunities by interacting with target language speakers. Ervin-Tripp (1970) comments on this fact by stating that how children learn a second language is largely dependent on the inner feelings of the learners themselves. She suggests it is not enough to focus on the opportunity itself without considering how learners make use of various social situations to develop linguistic competence in the second language. It follows that the more children practice, the better their competence should become. Students who are motivated to intensively interact in the second language learn at a faster rate than those who are passive.

The degree to which children are motivated to become actively involved in potential practice situations to learn the second language is revealed in the strategy called **Choosing the Way.** This affective strategy illustrates children's preferred modes of participation in second-language learning. Individual differences, including egocentric, attitudinal, and social factors, reflect the reality that language learning is a highly personal activity that is greatly influenced by children's motivational style.

Choosing the Way complements the cognitive learning approach seen in the strategy Putting It Together in that it describes children's affective or motivational style of acquiring a second language. Brown (1972) states that although the cognitive approach is important in understanding second-language learning, equally important is the approach taken from the viewpoint of the psychological or affective domain. The Office of Civil Rights Lau Guidelines includes in its second requirement a direction to school systems to consider both cognitive and affective aspects of how children learn a second language. It is only when children's affective or motivational style is considered along with their cognitive style that real insights and understanding of the total process of second-language learning are derived.

The motivational styles children reveal in their approach to second-language learning are as distinct as their cognitive styles. Motivational styles may facilitate cr impede language learning. While children may have all the cognitive factors to learn a second language, their progress may be retarded because of lack of motivation or an affective block. Some children manifest this affective block in terms of their negative attitude toward making use of practice opportunities to learn the second language.

Children enter school deeply and exclusively identified with their parents, with whom they share a culture. The psychological fusion between children and their parents results from shared experiences, values, and traditions. Children are socialized in a milieu that is permeated with a sense of belonging. Children's identities are formed through close association with parents and their belief systems. Children become comfortable with the identity they develop as parents reinforce their sense of who they are through consistent patterns of interaction.

The school is the first milieu children enter outside the home. For many minority children, the sociocultural context of the home and the neighborhood is very different from that of the mainstream socioculture of the school. The difference is greater in some families than in others. When the school milieu is very different from the home environment both linguistically and culturally, children experience what has been termed a "psychosocial identity crisis." (Erikson 1968) This is characterized by a sense of confusion, alienation, and discomfort. Children feel confused by a language that they don't understand. They feel alienated by dominant language speakers who may initially reject socializing attempts and exclude these children from their in-group. Thus, children who have previously felt very much a part of a family and neighborhood group suddenly feel like outsiders who don't belong. In addition, children experience discomfort in having to relate to new values and traditions which they may interpret as undermining family ideals. For example, whereas children's families may place great value on group interaction, the school often reflects conversely a culture that rewards individual initiative. Children feel under pressure to conform so that they may become part of the school culture.

Conformity entails taking on not only a new language but a new culture and value system. Children are faced with having to develop functional adaptation to two sets of environments, the home and the school. Each environment may have different sets of functional demand characteristics. Children feel overwhelmed and disoriented when there is little overlap between the home and the school. In an attempt to maintain continuity and preserve their personal sense of integrity these children adapt to the school environment in different ways: by identifying with the school culture and rejecting their home culture, by maintaining their native language identity, or by trying to integrate the two value systems in a bicultural identity. Thus, school entrance becomes a turning point in identity formation for these children. Erikson (1968) describes this psychological identity crisis as "a necessary turning point, when development must move one way or another, marshaling resources for growth and further differentiation of identity or by maintaining and rigidifying the present identity." The motivation of children to identify with the second culture or to crystalize their native language identity is closely related to their attitudes toward second-language speakers (Lambert 1967). Children who are strongly motivated to learn the language have a desire to identify with English speakers. Conversely, motivation to learn a second language is weak when children lack the desire to identify with second-language speakers: these children interpret this identification as being a threat to their first-language identity.

Three distinct motivational styles reflect the preferred modes of participation in second-language learning which minority children choose to adopt in an attempt to resolve their psychosocial identity crisis. The first motivational style is labeled **Crystalizing.** Children manifesting this style choose to maintain their identity with the native language culture and to initially reject the second language. Secondly, there is the motivational style termed **Crossing Over.** Children who adopt this style decide to identify with the second culture in preference to the first. Finally, there is the motivational style named **Crisscrossing.** This style is characterized by children who have harmonious identification with both first and second cultures.

Motivational styles are intimately tied with language pattern use. For example, children who reveal the Crisscrossing motivational style are likely to practice both languages. Children who identify primarily with the second-language group, Crossovers, are likely to adopt language use patterns that promote the replacement of the first language with the second. Crystalizers, who reject the second culture, will be resistant to learning the second language and will continue in communication patterns with peers who speak their native language.

Laosa (1975) examined the use of language patterns in specific social contexts of 295 first, second, and third-grade Hispanic children from three distinct ethnic and geographic groups: Texas—Mexican Americans, New York—Puerto Ricans, and Miami—Cubans. Contextual use of language patterns was obtained by individual interviews with children, mothers, and teachers. Questions were designed to solicit information describing the total amount of time spent by the students in verbal behavior in the first and second language. Teachers were asked about language patterns used by children in two school contexts: in classrooms during instruction, and in spontaneous interactions with peers outside formal classroom time. The resultant language patterns were identified as: English as the single language used most often,

Spanish as the language verbalized most frequently, and both English and Spanish spoken with equal frequency. These patterns of language use have also been described by Cummins (1979) and Lambert and Peal (1976).

The fact that children adopt one of these three patterns of language use is confirmed by the foregoing studies; however, the reasons why children choose one pattern over another has not been explained. Only by carefully examining the psychological or affective domain of language learning through the identification of divergent egocentric, attitudinal, and social motivational factors can we begin to understand why children adopt one pattern of verbal interaction over another. Unique personality variables lead children to choose a particular motivational style and this choice affects children's initial second-language learning.

The first motivational style to be considered is Crystalizing. The attitude of children who adopt this pattern of language use is exemplified by María. María, in response to Miguel's pleading for her to "C'mon over and play" with the English speakers, replies, "No, quiero quedarme aquí con Rosa, Maricela y Carlos." (No, I want to stay here with Rosa, Maricela and Carlos.) María further explains her statement to Miguel by asserting her preference for playing with her own friends instead of with the other children. "Prefiero jugar con mis propios amigos. No quiero jugar con los otros niños." (I'd rather play with my own friends. I don't want to play with the other children.) María's responses manifest the high positive value she places on her first language and culture. She construes speaking Spanish as a marker of group membership. The ideological affiliation she has with native language speakers takes precedence over participation in the second language and culture. María's desire is to maintain Spanish as her most frequent language pattern for social interactions.

The exclusivity that María exhibits by clearly stating that she prefers native language speakers also reflects her attitude toward English speakers. María chooses to set herself apart from English-speaking peers. She does not want to socially interact or identify with them and so refuses to cross over and play with the English speakers. María thus crystalizes her native language identity by standing firm in her position not to participate in opportunities to learn the new language and culture.

María's stance also reflects her personality characteristics. María appears to be very self-critical. It is very important to her that she maintain her dignity and pride. She refuses to speak English until she can do so without error. María doesn't like the uncertainty of perhaps not being able to express herself in a social interaction with English speakers. For this reason she opts to socialize in her native language, where she can communicate effectively and easily. This fact is reflected in María's statement to Miguel, "No sé decir las cosas que quiero en inglés." (I don't know how to say the things I want to in English.) María's position not to speak English until she is comfortable is further depicted when, even after Miguel offers to help her to communicate in English, saying, "Yo puedo ayudarte." (I can help you), María remains adamant. She repeats, "No, quiero quedarme aquí." (No, I want to stay here.)

In the classroom, children who adhere to the Crystalizing motivational style are best characterized as passive second-language learners. Their behavior may be reactive to input but they do little to initiate situations which cause more input to be directed to them. These children tend to interact inside and outside the classroom primarily with others who speak their mother tongue. They communicate with the teacher in English only when prodded during structured lessons. As passive learners they do not exploit practice opportunities but, as demonstrated, retreat and avoid socializing with English speakers. These children are therefore highly dependent on classroom activities which structure discourse in English for practicing the language.

The previously mentioned study by Seliger and Gingras (1976) on language contact and motivation labels these passive learners as "low input generators." Low input generators are described as: receiving a limited amount of focused input in the second language, not seeking out practice opportunities in the language, and as displaying avoidance behaviors toward second-language speakers. Crystalizers, as low input generators, have little motivation to take advantage of opportunities to participate in second-language communicative encounters. They instead sit quietly on the periphery of the group, contributing little to English discussions unless specifically asked by the teacher to do so.

Crystalizers approach language learning slowly and cautiously. Expressive English language usage is restricted to those statements which they can make confidently without error. Spontaneous verbalization in English is obviously missing. In large groups these students rarely volunteer answers. When they do respond to a directed question, Crystalizers appear to be analyzing or translating before speaking. They at times repeat words they hear very softly, often in tones inaudible to a person more than a few feet away. Utterances are typically shorter and briefer than other children's.

The emphasis in second-language learning is clearly placed by Crystalizers on the receptive understanding of the second language rather than on expressive verbalization. They are listening participants in language learning, engaging in long periods of silent observation until the entire code is absorbed before speaking. Perfection in comprehension is expected before a commitment is made to verbalization.

Crystalizers can be described as cautious learners who acquire the language best through successive approximation techniques. Language learning for them often involves four sequential steps: 1) receptive understanding of the second language 2) sequential testing of individual words 3) use of language in paired or small-group, lesson-related classroom activities 4) verbalization in the second language for social interactions.

The fact that Crystalizers express themselves socially in the second language as the final step is a result of their persistence in code switching to the native language for social encounters. This may be due to an insecurity and unfamiliarity with both the language and culture that causes them to fear interacting with those whom they don't know intimately or socially as members of their minority group. When Crystalizers do begin speaking to English peers they initially attend to how well their speech is being received and whether their performance meets with learned receptive standards.

Crystalizers as a rule have reserved personalities. They are basically shy children who take a long time to "warm up" to new people. They usually have a few close friends whom they cling to for support. Attachment to family is usually very strong.

Cognitively, they usually display a Beading approach to language learning. Because they have this analytical cognitive style as well as a passive motivational attitude toward second-language learning, they learn language more slowly—one word at a time. As Savignon (1972) notes, "learners that are cautious in their attitudes toward the second language may initially be less successful." Learning is blocked for these children because of their tendency to avoid situations in which they must communicate in English. They resist speaking the second language because it is something new which will force them to change their usual style of communication, a style that is extremely familiar and comfortable to them.

The motivational style of Crystalizing can be summed up as a passive attitude toward second-language learning. Children with this motivational style have personality characteristics that predispose them to hold back from speaking the language until they are totally confident. These students value speaking correctly over communicating for the sake of social interaction. They react to the psychosocial identity crisis by tenaciously holding onto and crystalizing their first language identity.

In direct contrast to Crystalizers are second-language learners whose motivational style can be termed "Crossing Over." Children with this style choose to actively pursue the learning of the second language even to the extent of giving up speaking the native language in the school setting. These students actively elicit stimulation and response from dominant language speakers. A dynamic ongoing interaction then takes place. By initiating and responding to language interaction with dominant speakers these children cause a reflexive response in the form of more language input to themselves.

The motivational style, Crossing Over, describes those students who make a deliberate effort to get second-language speakers to use the language with them. They seem to intuitively sense that they are dependent on language knowers in the environment to provide them with appropriate models (Seliger 1977). These students don't sit and wait to be addressed but rather seek out dominant speakers to relate to them and feed them the language. Crossovers are children who are able to capitalize on practice opportunities both in and out of the classroom. There is less dependence on language learning from structured drills and more on inducing language from natural social contexts. Braiding cognitive style is noted frequently with these learners who are motivated to continually pick up chunks of language and imitate them in formal and informal settings.

Children with the Crossover motivational style have numerous interactions with English speakers. Seliger (1977) points out that the total number of interactions correlates with rapidity of second-language learning. Therefore, the end result of the Crossing Over motivational approach is a second-language competence which develops at a faster and perhaps qualitatively better rate. By getting more focused input, Crossovers are able to test more hypotheses about the shape and use of the second language.

The term Crossing Over also symbolizes the attitude of children toward the second language. Students who choose this participant structure of interaction project a positive attitude, an admiration, and warmth toward English speakers. They are not so emotionally committed to their first language that they are unwilling to accommodate to the new language and culture. These students may, in fact, value the second language over their first, believing that it serves many cognitive and social functions in the school setting. The high value placed on the second language is made apparent by an overriding impetus to strongly identify with second-language speakers. This identification may signify an inner emancipation from their minority group affiliation. Crossovers, in fact, detach themselves at least temporarily from native language speaking peers in favor of socializing with English speakers. They choose to address the psychosocial identity crisis by negating their first-language identity and crossing over to assume a new identity with the second language and culture.

Personality variables of this motivational style include: flexibility, impulsiveness, and a sense of independence. Flexibility is noted as Crossovers assimilate the second language and culture into their currently existing psychological structures and modify these structures by accommodating to the demands of the new environment, thus evolving in cognitive and social functioning (Laosa 1979). Children with this style view identifications with the second language as tools for successful adaptation to the school environment. Impulsivity is expressed by Crossovers' willingness to take chances. They jump right into a series of social encounters without analyzing the situations or their competence to interact in English. They remain unflustered even when they have difficulty expressing themselves. A sense of independence is revealed by these children's self-assertiveness. From the beginning stages of second-language learning, these children adopt an attitude of personal responsibility for their own learning. They appear uninhibited, displaying a relaxed and open attitude.

Miguel is characterized by the Crossing Over motivational style. He is anxious to play with the English speakers. He does not remain with María when she refuses to cross over. He expresses an independence in his statement, "Entonces, me voy." (Then I'm going.) He does not want to hang back. He wants to venture out into the English speech community. He crosses over to join the English speakers with a sense of confidence. In doing this he cuts himself adrift from first-language peers.

Setting themselves apart from native language speakers seems to be one technique to gain linguistic competence used by children with this style. It is as if they feel immersion in the second language to the exclusion of the first is the most expedient way of quickly developing proficiency. Exploration of the new language includes establishing social ties with English speakers. Abrupt transformation distinguishes the Crossing Over style from that of Crystalizing, which is marked by gradual change. As Crossovers, children demonstrate a form and flow to learning which is constant. Active language learning is the key element.

The third motivational style is termed Crisscrossing. Children who espouse this participant structure habitually switch between the two languages and cultures. They often verbalize by mixing the two languages. Cornejo (1974) describes this mixing as the use of grammatical, lexical, and phonological aspects of both English and Spanish within single sentences. There is not only a mixing of English and Spanish within sentences but a predominance of code switching that is noticed as children express themselves in different cultural settings. Crisscrossers socialize between groups of native language and English speakers. No preference is shown for one group over the other. Unlike Crystalizers, they do not cling exclusively to their native language; neither do they abandon it in favor of English as do children with the Crossing Over style.

Crisscrossers have a positive attitude toward both the first and second language and hence teeter-totter between the two. They seem to want to integrate a wide range of experience into their social repertoire by interacting with both cultural groups. There is a constant comparing and contrasting that is noted as students try out phrases gathered through communicative encounters. When Crisscrossers have difficulty expressing themselves in one language they borrow from the other. Given the fact that these children are comfortable borrowing back and forth, they don't approach the second language as intensely as Crossovers and thus initially don't achieve the latter's proficiency in English. On the other hand, Crisscrossers do not take the passive attitude of Crystalizers and consequently outpace these children in initial expressive language use.

Crisscrossers' personality variables include versatility, adaptability, and spontaneity. Versatility is expressed in Crisscrossers' ability to easily switch back and forth between languages and cultures. Students with this style transfer language and cultural mannerisms from one culture to the other.

Their adaptability is noted in their case of expression. Crisscrossers appear to feel comfortable in new situations and adjust their communication patterns appropriately. Social expression is of primary importance to them, as is the flow of conversation. This flow is maintained through the insertion of a first language word for an unknown label in English. Translation is another important learning strategy. Crisscrossers frequently rely on bilinguals to translate messages to English-dominant peers. Spontaneity is revealed in quickness of response. Sometimes the responses in English seem initially somewhat incoherent. Poor sequential arrangement of borrowed words from both languages contributes to this incoherence.

Crisscrossers react to the psychosocial identity crisis by formulating a bicultural identity. In doing this, Crisscrossers don't give up their native language or culture but instead maintain it and adopt a second-language identity as well. They switch back and forth between identities. They settle ultimately on cultural consolidation and accommodation as an approach to second-language learning.

Children differ along the motivation continuum in their desire to identify with English speakers. Identifying with English-speaking peers involves a process of simultaneous reflection and observation, a process taking place on all levels of mental and emotional functioning (Jung 1974). Children "choose the way" of identifying or not identifying with the second language and culture. This choice is influenced by children's attitudes, emotions, and personality characteristics and is manifested in their motivational style. Children who choose to reject their first language and culture in favor of identifying with English speakers have what has been termed the Crossing Over motivational style. Children who choose to maintain their first language identity reveal a Crystalizing style. Finally, those children who develop a bicultural identity are described by the Crisscrossing motivational style. Identification choices expressed by motivational style explain how children choose to resolve the psychosocial identity crisis which results from the discontinuities between the native language and culture and the second language and culture as well as the split between the home and the school. The way children choose to resolve the identity issue predisposes them to participate actively or passively in second-language learning.

IMPLICATIONS OF CHOOSING THE WAY
FOR SECOND-LANGUAGE LEARNING
AND CLASSROOM TEACHING

The concept of motivational style defines the attitudinal and emotional factors which influence children's progress in learning the second language. Style determines whether the language is approached with tremor or bravado. It is important to note that no one motivational style is better than another. Children with all three styles learn the second language eventually. Motivational styles clarify, however, the personality and attitudinal characteristics which permit some children to progress more quickly than others. The teacher who understands how children differ in their approaches to language learning can plan and structure activities that ensure optimum learning for each style. Instruction in this way can center around the personalities and feelings of the learners rather than around a mechanical, programmed approach.

The teacher's sensitivity toward children will highly influence how activities are individualized. The approach taken will reflect how the teacher is motivated to consider alternative methods of second-language learning opportunities for students. Motivational style must thus be understood not only as mirroring students' personality make-up but also as reflecting the teacher's disposition or temperament—a two-way process. Teachers are motivated to react to children according to teacher personalities. The words of the teacher are clothed in the teacher's personality and indicate his or her expectations and perceptions. The teacher's language and behavior communicate to students an understanding of these students as individuals. An awareness of children's personalities is manifested by a variety of activities that are initiated or encouraged by the teacher in the classroom. Sensitivity is also noted in interpersonal relationships of teachers with students. The teacher's relationship with students should be recognized as a major determinant in second-language learning. The teacher is the primary model of the second language and culture. The more children can positively identify with their teacher (as well as with their English-speaking peers), the easier the adjustment will be to the new language and culture.

The identification process between teacher and student is reinforced when the teacher assumes a social role with children in addition to that of intellectual mentor. The school day should be structured to permit time for the teacher to socialize with students. Conversations between teacher and student should be unstructured and flow naturally from the social encounter. One teacher made it an active practice to engage in conversation with children during an art activity period. An example of this natural communicative encounter is noted in the following:

Teacher: That bunny you're drawing is very fat.
Student: It's a mommy bunny. All mommy bunnies are fat.
Teacher: Well, maybe she should go on a diet.
Student: Yea, my mommy's got a diet. She eats only . . . you know.
Teacher: I should go on a diet too, but I like cookies too much.
Student: You like cookies! Me too! Chocolate chip—big ones!

In this conversation, the teacher built on the child's statements in the form of a social dialogue. A sense of rapport was developed between teacher and student as they shared their liking for cookies. The student was, in a sense, amazed that the teacher actually liked cookies. (You like cookies!) Often teachers don't realize that children, especially young children, don't see them as real human beings with needs and wants just as they have. By building on social dialogue, the teacher allows children to perceive him or her as a fellow human being with whom they can identify. Social communication lays the foundation for this identification process between student and teacher.

As the teacher converses socially with individual children, she or he will become more acutely aware that children respond according to their personality and motivational style. Crystalizers may initially be very reticent, replying in monosyllables. Crossovers will chatter on and on, loving the social encounter. Crisscrossers will verbalize in sentences that will include words from both languages, often asking the teacher for translation of native language words. Regardless of how children initially respond to the teacher, he or she can be sure that the children have benefited in their own unique way from the social encounter.

The acceptance of students as individuals with unique personalities that influence their language learning can be further addressed by the teacher through the harmonious matching of motivational style with instructional and social strategies. The Crystalizing style responds best to lessons which are based on the receptive understanding of language. Tapes accompanied by activities, stories, and songs may be listened to by Crystalizers until an ease of understanding is gained. When once this receptive ability is developed, expressive language initially can best be encouraged through lessons that stress choral response. These lessons allow Crystalizers to participate yet not feel uncomfortable by being singled out. Social use of language can be stimulated through the "buddy system." This method pairs Crystalizers with English-language speakers for structured and unstructured play activity. The success of this technique depends on the teacher's perceptiveness in arranging congenial pairs. Crystalizers should be paired with English-speakers who take an active interest in others, even a "mothering" approach, rather than an overly aggressive stance. Children having similar play interests also can be successfully paired.

Crystalizers must be made to feel comfortable with the environment. They are usually at war with themselves in terms of trying to establish some continuity between the home and school milieus. Successful adaptation to the school environment is impeded if it is too abruptly different or different in critical ways from that of the home. In the face of real discontinuities, Crystalizers may give up trying and rigidify in first-language identity. Rigidity does not allow for synthesis, and thus, children fail to progress to higher levels of integration and to make the transition to the new language and culture.

The teacher helps Crystalizers adjust to the second language and culture by examining those aspects of the school environment that are most discontinuous with the home. Once these elements have been noted, an articulated continuity needs to be established between the sociocultural contexts of home and school. This continuity is manifested as two-way understanding between cultures. The teacher can facilitate this two-way understanding by making a concentrated effort to discover how school language meshes with home language variables such as: content and tone, cultural patterns, aspirations, and values. Too often the cultural background and values of children from ethnic minorities are just as foreign to teachers as the second-language culture is to these students.

The loyalty, emotional attachment, and strong identification Crystalizers feel toward their first language and culture causes them to initially distrust affiliation with second-language speakers. They feel somehow that learning the second language will displace their first. These children can be made to feel more comfortable with the second language and their feelings of distrust can be diminished by the teacher who involves these children's and other children's families in school activities. A "Family Day" should be planned at the beginning of the year to establish immediate contact with the home. Family Day should then be built upon throughout the year by inviting families to the school for social and cultural events. Class discussion meetings can involve students in sharing with their parents what they are learning in the classroom. Parents can also be asked to participate in teaching and skill-sharing with children in the class. There is a sense of pride that children feel in seeing their parents teach their peers.

Community planned parent advisory committees have been established at many schools to allow parents to participate in educational planning for their children. Late afternoon or evening ESL classes at the school can enable parents to learn the language along with their children. The teacher who establishes some continuity between the home and the school will find that students, especially those with a Crystalizing motivational style, will be less fearful of participating in language learning opportunities. Parents who are made to feel part of the school community will become the teacher's allies in supporting their children in the language learning process.

The teacher's ultimate success in getting Crystalizers involved in second-language learning will be through indirect methods, such as arranging social-communicative pairs or through family involvement. Crystalizers enter the second culture gradually, as an end result of small steps. They are most amenable to systematic influence. The teacher can facilitate learning for these children by not exerting pressure on them to speak before they are ready, by establishing some continuity between first versus second culture, and, most importantly, by the process of positive identification experiences, making them comfortable as a member of two cultures.

Crossovers are encouraged by the teacher to learn the second language when they are given freedom and the opportunity to interact with English speakers both in and out of the classroom. Crossovers should be exposed to a combination of structured and unstructured English-learning activities. Structured activities include meaningful pattern drill, vocabulary development, and problem solving activities. Unstructured activities include planting seeds, hatching chicks or local outings where language flows from the natural social context.

Crossovers particularly benefit from exposure to large numbers of English-speaking models, including adults as well as children. Exposure to a large number of models has a facilitative effect on second-language learning, especially vocabulary. Crossovers who have a high level of drive to identify with English speakers benefit greatly from diverse language models. Learning the second language from a variety of language models permits children to acquire a broader range of social expressions and vocabulary with which they can extend their English repertoire. Thus, the teacher should encourage parents and other members of the school and the community to serve as language models for children. This can be done by having English-speaking parents work with small groups of children or by inviting English speakers to engage in social dialogue with children in the form of a planned activity.

Crossovers should also be involved in structuring some of their second-language learning experiences. These children seem to intuitively know how to structure their social experiences to learn the second language. They rely on inner guides for action rather than on the external cues provided by the teacher. The teacher need only become aware of the types of activities that stimulate Crossovers to use language and then reinforce these activities. Crossovers make the greatest progress in classrooms where English is integrated into the total school program in terms of academic work and extracurricular activities.

The teacher can build on the motivational style of Crisscrossers by assisting them in orchestrating first and second language patterns into two separate linguistic systems. Crisscrossers must be made aware of the differences and similarities between each language which exist at a functional as well as at a structural level. Awareness develops as the teacher gives feedback to students in structured and unstructured situations on the correct linking of vocabulary and grammatical configurations for each language. Initial learning can be facilitated for Crisscrossers by stressing grammatical patterns that overlap languages. This enables children to draw rules from a single grammar pool. Conscious control over structures and the ability to manipulate them in both languages will aid children who are motivated to become bilingual.

Instructional focus for Crisscrossers should center on functional communication in each language that does not depend on language mixing. Clear separation of languages by time, location, or speaker dissuades Crisscrossers from communicating with fragments from each language and strengthens their ability to use each linguistic system holistically.

Classroom instruction can differentiate between languages by presenting certain subjects in each particular language. Duplicating subjects in both languages is counterproductive. Rather, subject disciplines should be divided by language for initial linguistic instruction. Reading can be taught first in the native language. There is some evidence that math processes are better retained in the language they were first learned. Thus, English instruction in math may stimulate long-term achievement for children in transitional bilingual programs. Finally, languages can be kept distinct for Crisscrossers through bilingual program options such as: the "Half Day Plan," in which the home language is taught for part of the day and English for the other, or the "Mixed Day Plan," where some subjects are taught in native language and others in English.

Children who are motivated to learn in both languages achieve most in a school program which attempts to promote cognitive and social usage of first and second language in the form of additive bilingualism. Classrooms that permit a wide range of social interactions across groups encourage children to add social expressions from each language to their linguistic repertoire. Cognitive development is promoted through structured learning opportunities that maintain the integrity of each language.

The discussion of motivational style is meant to give teachers insights into approaches that individualize second-language learning opportunities for students. By becoming sensitive to children's attitudes toward the second language and culture, the teacher can determine what blocks and what accelerates learning. The teacher can answer questions such as: Is language learning blocked by internal fears or is it due to the method of presentation? Answers to these questions enable the teacher to concentrate on giving emotional support to fearful children or to modify teaching approaches.

Individualization in ESL instruction takes account of the fact that students with diverse motivational styles respond differently to methods of teaching. There are some approaches to which one style of learner can readily adapt yet with which another style of learner must struggle. Teachers concerned with individualization create learning situations through which students can acquire the second language most comfortably and easily. One method of individualization is to divide the room into learning centers that correspond to motivational styles such as:

Listening Area — (Crystalizers)

Group Activities — desks grouped together (Crossovers)

Vocabulary Activities — divided in two sections by language (Crisscross-
          crossers)

These centers present children with diverse language learning opportunities.

Teachers, as the prime motivators in the classroom, encourage all children to learn English as a second language by expressing confidence in children's ability to succeed and by demonstrating a warmth and understanding of children's first language and culture. Finally, by serving as a model of the second language and culture, the teacher encourages English language learning through the identification process.

Bibliography

Abrahams, R.D. A performance-centered approach to gossip. *Man* 5 (1979): 290–301.

Ager, D.E. Language learning and sociolinguistics. *IRAL* 14, 3 (August 1976): 285–295.

Altman, H.B. The language connection, or talk is not always cheap. *Foreign Language Annals* (1978): 359–365.

Anderson, N. The uses and worth of language. *Studies in Bilingualism.* Edited by N. Anderson. The Netherlands: E.J. Brill, 1969.

Anderson, R.W. An implicational model for second-language research. *Language Learning* 28, 2 (1978): 221–229.

Applegate, R.B. The language teacher and the rules of speaking. *TESOL Quarterly* 9, 3 (September 1975): 271–281.

Asher, J.J. The learning strategy of the total physical response: a review. *The Modern Language Journal* 50, 2 (1966): 79–84.

_____ Children's first language as a model for second-language learning. *The Modern Language Journal* (March 1972): 221–229.

Asher, S.R. Children's ability to appraise their own and another person's communication performance. *Developmental Psychology* 12 (1976): 24–32.

Asher, S.R. and Parke, R.D. Influence of sampling and comparison processes on the development of communication effectiveness. *Journal of Educational Psychology* 67, 1 (1975): 64–75.

Baker, J.A. Interdisciplinary, grade-level terms from jargon to reality. *Middle School Journal* 7, 1 (March 1976): 10–11.

Barclay, J.R.; Bransford, J.D.; Franks, J.J.; McCarrell, N.S.; and Nitsch, K. Comprehension and semantic flexibility. *Journal of Verbal Learning and Verbal Behavior* 13 (1974): 471–481.

Beebe, L.M. The influence of the listener on code-switching. *Language Learning* 27 (December 1977): 331–339.

Bennett, C. Teaching students as they would be taught: the importance of cultural perspective. *Educational Leadership* (January 1979): 259–268.

Ben-Zeev, S. The effect of Spanish-English bilingualism in children from less privileged neighborhoods on cognitive development and cognitive strategy. Unpublished research report to National Institute of Child Health and Human Development, 1975.

_____ Mechanisms by which childhood bilingualism affects understanding of language and cognitive structures. *Bilingualism: Psychological, Social, and Educational Implications*. Edited by P.A. Hornby. New York: Academic Press, 1977.

Bergold, S. Children's growth of competence in storytelling. *Language Arts* 53, 6 (September 1976): 658–662.

Berko-Gleason, J. Code-switching in children's language. *Cognitive Development and the Acquisition of Language*. Edited by T.E. Moore. New York: Academic Press, 1973.

Berkowitz, M. Mother of twenty-two holds press conference. *Elementary English* 49, 6 (October 1972): 898–900.

Bernstein, B. Social structure, language and learning. *Educational Research* 3 (1961): 163–176.

Bialystok, E. A theoretical model of second-language learning. *Language Learning* 28, 1 (1978): 69–83.

Blom, J.P. and Gumperz, J.J. Social meaning in linguistic structure: code-switching in Norway. *Directions in Sociolinguistics*. Edited by J.J. Gumperz and D. Hymes. New York: Holt, Rinehart and Winston, 1973.

Bloom, L. *Language Development*. Cambridge, Mass.: MIT Press, 1970.

_____ Language development. *Review of Child Development Research (Volume 4)*. Edited by F.D. Horowitz. Chicago: University of Chicago Press, 1975.

Bloom, L.; Hood, L.; and Lightbown, P. Imitation in language development: if, when, and why. *Cognitive Psychology* 6 (1974): 380–420.

Bloomfield, L. *Language*. New York: Henry Holt and Co., 1933.

Boggs, S.T. and Watson-Gegeo, K.A. Interweaving routines: strategies for encompassing a social situation. *Language in Society* 7, 3 (December 1978): 375–392.

Bourgere, H.B. Selected factors in oral language related to first-grade reading achievement. *Reading Research Quarterly* (Fall 1969): 31–57.

Bransford, J.E. and Franks, J.J. The abstraction of linguistic ideas. *Cognitive Psychology* 2 (1971): 331–350.

Brend, R.M. Politeness. *IRAL* 16, 3 (1978): 253–256.

Brenneis, D. and Lein, L. Children's disputes in three speech communities. *Language in Society* 7 (1978): 299–323.

Briere, E. Quantity before quality in second-language composition. *Language Learning* 16 (1966): 141–151.

Britton, J. *Language and Learning.* London: Penguin Books, 1970.

Brown, G.W. Words and things. *Journal of Learning Disabilities* 5, 10 (November 1972): 61–63.

Bruner, J.S. Cognitive guessing strategies. *Human Development* 13 (1970): 149–177.

——— Early childhood education: preliminaries to a theory of cultural differences. *National Society for the Study of Education: Part 2* 13 (1972): 161–179.

——— From communication to language: a psychological perspective. *Cognition* 3 (1974-75): 283.

Bruner, J.S. and Kenney, H.J. Representation and mathematics learning. *Monographs of the Society for Research in Child Development.* Edited by L.N. Morrison and J. Vinsonhaler. 30, 1, Serial No. 99 (1965): 50–59.

Burns, A.T. and Guilford, P.D. Wakulla county oral language project. *Elementary English* (1969): 611–616.

Burt, M. and Dulay, H., eds. *New Directions in Second-Language Learning and Teaching.* Washington, D.C.: TESOL, 1975.

Butler, L.G. Language acquisition of young children: major theories and sequences. *Elementary English* 50 (November-December 1973): 1120–1123.

Campbell, D.E. and Campbell, T.A. Effects of live and recorded storytelling on retelling performance of preschool children from low socioeconomic backgrounds. *Psychology in the Schools* 13, 2 (April 1976): 201–204.

Campbell, R. English curricula for non-English speakers. *Monograph Series of Languages and Linguistics.* Edited by J.E. Alatis. Washington, D.C.: Georgetown University Press, 1970.

Carlton-Caprio, D. Learning by doing: a practical foreign language classroom experience. *Modern Language Journal* (March 1975): 97–100.

Carroll, J.B. Foreign languages for children: what research says. *National Elementary Principal* 39, 6 (1960): 12–15.

——— Psychological and educational research into second-language teaching to young children. *Language and the Young School Child.* Edited by H.H. Stern. London: Oxford University Press, 1969.

——— Development of native language skills beyond the early years. *The Learning of Language.* Edited by C.E. Reed. Englewood Cliffs, N.J.: Prentice-Hall, 1971.

——— Some suggestions from a psycholinguist. *TESOL Quarterly* 7, 4 (1973): 355–367.

Carter, A.L. The development of communication in the sensorimotor period: a case study. Ph.D. dissertation. University of California, Berkeley, 1974.

Carton, A.S. The method of inference in foreign language study. The Research Foundation of the City of New York, 1966.

Cawley, M. Connecting words with real ideas. *Young Children* (January 1978): 20–25.

Cazden, C.B. Play and metalinguistic awareness: one dimension of language experience. *The Urban Review* 7 (January 1974): 28–39.

Cazden, C.B.; Cox, M.; Dickinson, D.; Steinberg, Z.; and Stone, C. "You all gonna hafta listen": peer teaching in a primary classroom. *Children's Language and Communication.* Edited by W.A. Collins. Twelfth Annual Minnesota Symposium on Child Psychology. Hillsdale, N.J.: Lawrence Erlbaum, 1979.

Cazden, C.B.; Hymes, D.; and John, V., eds. *Functions of Language in the Classroom.* New York: Teachers College Press, Columbia University, 1972.

Champagne, D.W. and Hines, J.F. Role-play simulation as a teaching strategy—suggestions for new uses. *Educational Technology* (August 1971): 58–60.

Chastain, Kenneth. Affective and ability factors in second-language acquisition. *Language Learning* 25, 1 (June 1975): 153–161.

Ching, D. Reading and language development in the bilingual child: an annotated bibliography. *Elementary English* 46 (May 1969): 622–628.

Chomsky, N. *Current Issues in Linguistic Theory.* The Hague: Mouton, 1964.

_____ Linguistic theory. *1966 Northern Conference Report.* Edited by R.G. Mead.

Christian, C. The analysis of linguistic and cultural differences: a proposed model. *Monograph Series on Language and Linguistics.* Edited by J.E. Alatis. Washington, D.C.: Georgetown University Press, 1970.

Clarke, D.D. The syntax of action. *Oxford Review of Education* 4, 3 (1978): 239–255.

Cohen, A. Mexican-American evaluational judgments about language varieties. *Linguistics* 136 (September 1974): 33–51.

_____ *A Sociolinguistic Approach to Bilingual Education.* Rowley, Mass.: Newbury House Publishers, 1975.

Cohen, S.A. *Teach Them All to Read.* New York: Random House, 1969.

Cole, L. Relationships between visual presentations and linguistic items in second-language teaching. *International Review of Applied Linguistics in Language Teaching* 14, 4 (1976): 339–350.

Coleman, J. Differences between experiential and classroom learning. *Experimental Learning: Rationale, Characteristics and Assessment.* Edited by M. Keeton. San Francisco: Jossey-Bass, 1976.

Coles, R. *Children in Crisis: A Study of Courage and Fear.* Boston: Little, Brown, and Co., 1967.

Cook, V.J. The analogy between first and second language learning. *International Review of Applied Linguistics in Language Teaching* 7 (1969): 207–216.

Cooper, R.L. and Greenfield, L. Language use in a bilingual community. *Modern Language Journal* 53 (1969): 166–172.

Cooper, R.L. and Fishman, J.A. The study of language attitudes. *Linguistics* (September 1974): 5–19.

Corder, S.P. *The Visual Element in Language Teaching.* New York: Longmans, 1966.

———— Error analysis, interlanguage and second-language acquisition. *Language Teaching and Linguistics* 8 (1975): 201–217.

Cornejo, R.J. Synthesis of theories and research of the effects of teaching in first and second languages: implications for bilingual education. New Mexico State University, University Park ERIC Clearinghouse on Rural Education and Small Schools. Sponsoring Agency: National Institute of Education (D-HEW) Washington, D.C., June 1974.

Corsini, D. The effect of nonverbal cues on the retention of kindergarten children. *Child Development* 40 (1969): 599–607.

Cortes, C.E. The societal curriculum and the school curriculum: allies or antagonists? *Educational Leadership* (April 1979): 475–479.

Coser, L.A. *The Functions of Social Conflict.* New York: The Free Press, 1956.

Crockenberg, S.; Bryant, B.; and Wilce, L. The effects of cooperatively and competitively structured learning environments on inter- and intrapersonal behavior. *Child Development* 47 (1976): 386–396.

Crockenberg, S. and Bryant, B. Socialization: the "implicit curriculum" of learning environments. *Journal of Research and Development in Education* 12, 1 (Fall 1978): 69–78.

Cross, D.; Baker, G.; and Stiles, L. *Teaching in a Multicultural Society.* New York: The Free Press, 1977.

Cruikshank, D.E. Logic in language. *Language Arts* (1975): 762–768.

Cummins, J. *The Influence of Bilingualism on Cognitive Growth: A Synthesis of Research Findings and Explanatory Hypotheses.* Dublin: St. Patrick's College, 1976.

———— Linguistic interdependence and the educational development of bilingual children. *Review of Educational Research* 49, 2 (Spring 1979): 222–251.

———— The cross-lingual dimensions of language proficiency: implications for bilingual education and the optimal age issue. *TESOL Quarterly* 14, 2 (June 1980): 175–187.

Curran, C.A. *Counseling-Learning: A Whole Person Model for Education.* New York: Grune and Stratton, 1972.

———— *Counseling-Learning in Second Language.* Illinois: Apple River Press, 1976.

Curry, N. and Arnaud, S. Cognitive implications in children's spontaneous role-play. *Theory Into Practice* 13, 4 (1974): 273–277.

Daehler, M.W.; Horowitz, A.B.; Wynns, F.C.; and Flavell, J.H. Verbal and nonverbal rehearsal in children's recall. *Child Development* 40 (1969): 443–452.

Davis, G. Let's be an ice-cream machine. *Journal of Creative Behavior* 7, 1 (1973): 37–53.

DeLaguna, G. *Speech: Its Function and Development.* Bloomington: Indiana University Press, 1963. First published by Oxford University Press, 1927.

DeStefano, J.S. and Rental, V. Language variation: perspectives for teachers. *Theory Into Practice* 14, 5 (1975): 328–337.

Dewey, J. *The Child and the Curriculum.* Chicago: University of Chicago Press, 1902.

Diller, K.C. Some new trends for applied linguistics and foreign language teaching in the United States. *TESOL Quarterly* 9, 1 (March 1975): 65–73.

Dillon, D.A. Perspectives—Michael Stubbs: language, schools, and classrooms. *Language Arts* (November-December 1979): 941–949.

Dillon, R.F. and Bittner, L.A. Analysis of retrieval cues and release from proactive inhibition. *Journal of Verbal Learning and Behavior* 14 (1975): 616–622.

Dittmer, A. Language is alive! (so what else is new?). *English Journal* 60, 9 (December 1978): 20–26.

Drake, D. Empowering children through bilingual/bicultural education. *Education Forum* 40, 2 (January 1976): 199–204.

Draper, P. Sex differences in cognitive styles: socialization and constitutional variables. *Council on Anthropological Education*, August, 1975.

Dunn, R.S. and Dunn, K.J. Learning styles/teaching styles: should they . . . can they . . . be matched? *Educational Leadership* (January 1979): 238–244.

Dunning, G.B. Research in nonverbal communication. *Theory Into Practice* (1975): 250–257.

Dweck, C.S.; Hill, K.T.; Redd, W.H.; Steinman, W.M.; and Parke, R.D. The impact of social cues on children's behavior. *Merrill-Palmer Quarterly* 21, 2 (1976): 83–92.

Ebbinghaus, H. *Uber das Gedachnis*. Leipzip: Duncker and Humblot, 1885. Translated edition: *Memory*. New York: Dover, 1964.

Eckman, B. Making valid nonverbal judgments. *English Journal* 66, 8 (November 1977): 72–74.

Edwards, A.D. Speech codes and speech variants: social class and task differences in children's speech. *Journal of Child Language* 3, 4 (June 1976): 247–265.

Eliot, J. Large-scale representation: some characterizations and educational implications. *Educational Leadership* (January 1979): 278–282.

Elkind, D. Piaget and Montessori. *Harvard Educational Review* 37 (1967): 535–545.

Ellis, S.S. Models of teaching: a solution to the teaching style/learning style dilemma. *Educational Leadership* (January 1979): 274–277.

Epstein, N. *Language, Ethnicity and the Schools*. Washington, D.C.: The George Washington University Press, 1978.

Erikson, Erik H. *Identity: Youth and Crisis*. New York: W.W. Norton and Co., 1968.

Ervin-Tripp, S. An analysis of the interaction of language, topic and listener. *Readings in Sociology of Language*. Edited by J. Fishman. The Hague: Mouton, 1968.

_____ Structure and process in language acquisition. *Twenty-First Annual Roundtable: Bilingualism and Language Contact*. Edited by J.E. Alatis. Washington, D.C.: Georgetown University Press, 1970.

_____ Is second-language learning like the first? *TESOL Quarterly* 8 (1974): 111–127.

_____ *Child Discourse*. Edited by S. Ervin-Tripp. New York: Academic Press, 1977.

Ervin-Tripp, S. and Osgood, C.E. Second-language learning and bilingualism. *Journal of Abnormal and Social Psychology* 49 (1954): 139–146.

Fanselow, J. and Light, R. *Bilingual, ESOL and Foreign Language Teacher Preparation: Models, Practices, Issues*. Washington, D.C.: Pantagraph Press, 1977.

Fathman, A.K. Age, language background and the order of acquisition of English structures. Paper read at TESOL conference, Los Angeles, 1975.

_____ Variables affecting the successful learning of English as a second language. *TESOL Quarterly* 10, 4 (December 1976): 433–441.

Feldman, C.F. Pragmatic features of natural language. Paper read at the Tenth Regional Meeting—Chicago Linguistic Society, 1974.

Feldman, C.F. and Wertsch, J.V. Context dependent properties of teachers' speech. *Youth and Society* 7, 3 (March 1976): 227–258.

Ferguson, C.A. Sociolinguistic research and practical applications. *Applied Sociolinguistics.* Edited by A. Verdoodt. Heidelberg: Julius Groos Verlag, 1974.

_____ The structure and use of politeness formulas. *Language in Society* 5 (August 1976): 137–151.

Fillmore, L.W. The second-time around: cognitive and social strategies in second-language acquisition. Ph.D. dissertation. Stanford University, 1976.

_____ Learning a second language: Chinese children in the American classroom. *Roundtable on Language and Linguistics: Current Issues in Bilingual Education.* Edited by J.E. Alatis. Washington, D.C.: Georgetown University Press, 1980.

Fine, G.A. Social components of children's gossip. *Journal of Communication* 27 (Winter 1977): 181–185.

Finocchiaro, M. *Teaching English as a Second Language.* New York: Harper Bros., 1958.

Fischer, B.B. and Fischer, L. Styles in teaching and learning. *Educational Leadership* (January 1979): 245–254.

Fishman, J.A. Bilingualism with and without diglossia: diglossia with and without bilingualism. *The Journal of Social Issues.* Edited by J. MacNamara. 23 (1967): 29–38.

_____ *Readings in the Sociology of Language.* The Hague: Mouton, 1968.

_____ The politics of bilingual education. *Monograph Series on Languages and Linguistics.* Edited by J.E. Alatis. Washington, D.C.: Georgetown University Press, 1970.

_____ *Sociolinguistics: A Brief Introduction.* Rowley, Mass.: Newbury House Publishers, 1971.

Flavell, J.H. *The Development of Role Taking and Communication Skills in Children.* New York: John Wiley and Sons, 1968.

French. R.L. Individualizing classroom communication. *Educational Leadership* (November 1970): 193–196.

_____ Analyzing and improving verbal communication: a model for in-service education. *Theory Into Practice* (1975): 305–314.

Friedman, H.S. Scientists snatch body language. Review of R. Rosenthal et al, *Sensitivity to Nonverbal Communication: The PONS Test. Contemporary Psychology* 25, 2 (1980): 123–124.

Furlong, V.A. and Edwards, A.D. Language classroom interaction: theory and data. *Educational Research* 19, 2 (February 1977): 122–128.

Furness, P. Try role-playing. *Today's Education* 69, 1 (February 1977): 94–95.

Gage, N.L., ed. *Teaching as a Linguistic Process in a Cultural Setting.* Panel 5, National Conference on Studies in Teaching, National Institute of Education, Washington, D.C., December 1974.

Gagne, R.M. *Essentials of Learning for Instruction*. Hinsdale, Ill.: Dryden Press, 1974.

Galloway, C.M. Nonverbal: the language of sensitivity. *Theory Into Practice* (1975): 227–230.

Gardner, R. and Lambert, W.E. Attitudes and motivation in second-language learning. Rowley, Mass.: Newbury House Publishers, 1972.

Gardner, R. and Smythe, P.C. Motivation and second-language acquisition. *Canadian Modern Language Journal* 31, 3 (January 1975): 218–230.

Gardner, R.; Smythe, P.C.; Clement, R.; and Gliksman, L. Second-language learning: a social psychological perspective. *Canadian Modern Language Review* (1976): 198–213.

Garnica, O.K. How children learn to talk. *Theory Into Practice* 14, 5 (1975): 299–305.

Garvey, C. and Hogan, R. Social speech and social interaction: egocentrism revisited. *Child Development* 44 (1973): 562–568.

Garvey, C. Some properties of social play. *The Merrill-Palmer Quarterly* 20 (1974): 163–180.

Gary, J.O. Delayed oral practice in initial stages of second-language learning. *New Directions in Second-Language Learning, Teaching and Bilingual Education*. Edited by M. Burt and H. Dulay. Washington, D.C.: TESOL, 1975.

Genishi, C. Rules for code switching in young Spanish-English speakers: an exploratory study of language socialization. Ph.D. dissertation. University of California, Berkeley, 1976.

Getzels, J.W. Socialization and education: a note on discontinuities. *Teachers College Record* 68, 3 (December 1966): 219–228.

Gibson, R.E. The strip story: a catalyst for communication. *TESOL Quarterly* 9, 2 (June 1975): 149–154.

Gleason, J.B. and Weintraub, S. The acquisition of routines in child language. *Language in Society* 5 (August 1976): 129–136.

Glucksberg, S.; Krauss, R.M.; and Weisberg, R. Referential communication in nursery children: method and some preliminary findings. *Journal of Experimental Child Psychology* 3 (1966): 333–342.

Goebes, D. and Shore, M.F. Some effects of bicultural and monocultural school environments on personality development. *American Journal of Orthopsychiatry* 48, 3 (July 1978): 398–407.

Goffman, E. *The Presentation of Self in Everyday Life*. New York: Doubleday and Co., 1959.

_____ *Behavior in Public Places*. Illinois: Free Press, 1963.

_____ *Relations in Public: Microstudies of the Public Order*. London: Penguin Books, 1971.

Gonzalez, G. Teaching bilingual children. *Bilingual Education: Current Perspectives (Volume 2) Linguistics*. Arlington, Va.: Center for Applied Linguistics, 1977.

Gordon, R.F. and Flavell, J.H. The development of intuitions about cognitive cueing. *Child Development* 48 (1977): 1027–1033.

Gottman, J.G. and Rasmussen, B. Social interaction, social competence and friendship in children. *Child Development* 46 (1975): 709–718.

Gough, P.B. The limitations of imitation: the problem of language acquisition. *New Directions in Elementary English.* Edited by A. Fraizer. Urbana, Ill.: National Council of Teachers of English, 1967.

Graham, C. *Jazz Chants for Children: Rhythms of American English through Chants, Songs and Poems.* New York: Oxford University Press, 1979.

Grant, Barbara M. and Henning, Dorothy Grant. *The Teacher Moves: An Analysis of Nonverbal Activity.* New York: Teachers College Press, Columbia University, 1971.

Grant, Carl A. Classroom socialization: the other side of a two-way street. *Educational Leadership* (April 1979): 470–473.

Grittner, Frank M., ed. Changing times and changing needs in second-language learners. *Learning a Second Language Seventy-Ninth Yearbook of the National Society for the Study of Education, Part II.* Chicago: Chicago University Press, 1980.

Guinn, Robert. Value clarification in the bicultural classroom. *Journal of Teacher Education* 1 (January-February 1977): 46–47.

Guiora, A.Z.; Brannon, R.C.L.; and Dull, C.Y. Empathy and second-language learning. *Language Learning* 22 (1972): 111–130.

Gumperz, John J. Linguistic and social interaction in two communities. *The Ethnography of Communication: American Anthropologist.* Edited by J.J. Gumperz and D. Hymes. 66 (1964): 137–153.

_____ Verbal strategies in multilingual communication. *Monograph Series on Languages and Linguistics.* Edited by J.E. Alatis. Washington, D.C.: Georgetown University Press, 1970.

_____ On the sociolinguistic significance of conversational code-switching. Working paper No. 46, Language-Behavior Laboratory, University of California, Berkeley, 1976.

Gumperz, John J. and Herasimchuk, E. The conversational analysis of social meaning: a study of classroom interaction. *Sociolinguistics: Current Trends and Prospects.* Edited by R. Shuy. Washington, D.C.: Georgetown University Press, 1972.

Gumperz, John J. and Hernandez, Chavez E. Bilingualism, bidialectalism and classroom interaction. *Language in Social Groups: Essays by John J. Gumperz.* Edited by A.S. Dil. Stanford, Calif.: Stanford University Press, 1972.

Gunderson, Barbara. Cooperative structure in the foreign language classroom. *Teaching for Tomorrow in the Foreign Language Classroom.* Edited by Reid E. Baker. Skokie, Ill.: National Textbook Co., 1978.

Hakuta, K. Becoming bilingual at age five: the story of Uguisu. B.A. honors thesis. Harvard University, Department of Psychology and Social Relations, 1975.

Halliday, M.A.K. The users and uses of language. *Readings in the Sociology of Language.* Edited by J.A. Fishman. The Hague: Mouton, 1968.

_____ Language structure and language function. *New Horizons in Linguistics.* Edited by J. Lyons. London: Penguin Books, 1970.

_____ *Explorations in the Functions of Language.* London: Edward Arnold, 1973.

_____ *Learning to Mean.* Australia: University Press, 1975.

Hammerly, Hector. Recent methods and trends in second-language teaching. *Modern Language Journal* (December 1971): 499–505.

Hanley, J.P.; Whitla, D.K.; Moo, E.W.; and Walter, A.S. *Curiosity/Competence/Community—An Evaluation of Man: A Course of Study.* Cambridge, Mass.: Social Studies Curriculum, Educational Development Center, Inc., 1970.

Harris, Adrienne E. Social dialectics and language: mother and child construct the discourse. *Human Development* 18 (1975): 80–95.

Hart, Betty. The use of adult cues to test the language competence of young children. *Journal of Child Language* 2 (1975): 105–124.

Hartup, Willard W. Peer relations: developmental implications and interaction in same- and mixed-age situations. *Young Children* XXXII (March 1977): 4–13.

Hatch, Evelyn. Studies in Second-Language Acquisition. Paper read at the Congress of Applied Linguistics, Copenhagen, August 1972.

_____ *Second-Language Acquisition: A Book of Readings.* Edited by E. Hatch. Rowley, Mass.: Newbury House Publishers, 1978.

Henry, Richard A. The individualization of instruction in ESL. *TESOL Quarterly* IX, 1 (March 1975): 31–40.

Hernandez, V. The teaching of Spanish and its relation with the teaching of Latin and modern foreign languages. *Yelmo* 12 (June-July 1973): 29–33.

Hodge, A.A. Techniques of teaching foreign language. *Babel* 6, 3 (October 1970): 17–19.

Hodge, R. Lewis. Interpersonal classroom communication through eye contact. *Theory Into Practice* (1975): 264–267.

Hoffman, Moses N.H. *The Measurement of Bilingual Background.* New York: Teachers College Press, Columbia University, 1934.

Holden, M.H. and MacGinitie, W. H. Children's Conceptions of Word Boundaries in Speech and Print. Unpublished manuscript, Teachers College, Columbia University, n.d. Shortened version in *Journal of Educational Psychology* 63 (1972): 551–557.

Holley, Freda M. and King, Janet K. Imitation and correction in foreign language learning. *Language Learning* (March 1972): 48–51.

Hollingsworth, Paul M. Let's improve listening skills. *Elementary English* 50 (November-December 1973): 1156–1157.

Hollomon, John W. A practical approach to assessing bilingualism in young Mexican-American children. *TESOL Quarterly* X, 4 (December 1976): 389–401.

Hollos, Marida and Beeman, William. The development of directives among Norwegian and Hungarian children: an example of communicative style in culture. *Language in Society* 7 (December 1978): 345–355.

Holmes, Janet and Brown, Dorothy F. Developing sociolinguistic competence in a second language. *TESOL Quarterly* X, 4 (December 1976): 423–431.

Hornby, Peter A. ed. *Bilingualism: Psychological, Social, and Educational Implications.* New York: Academic Press, 1977.

Houston, S. A sociolinguistic consideration of Black English of children in northern Florida. *Language* 45 (1969): 599–607.

Huang, Joseph. A Chinese child's acquisition of English syntax. M.A. thesis, University of California, Los Angeles, 1971.

Hubbard, Louise J. Aptitude, attitude and sensitivity. *Foreign Language Annuals* (March 1975): 33–37.

Hunter, Diana Lee. Spoken and written word lists: a comparison. *Reading Teacher* 29, 3 (December 1975): 250–253.

Hymes, D.H. Directions in ethno-linguistic theory. *American Anthropologist* 66, 3 (1964): Part 2.

_____ Models of the interaction of language and social setting. *The Journal of Social Issues.* 23 (1967): 8–28.

_____ *Bilingual Education: Linguistic vs. Sociolinguistic Bases.* Washington, D.C.: Georgetown University Press, 1970.

_____ *Language in Social Groups.* Stanford, Calif.: Stanford University Press, 1971.

_____ On linguistic theory, communicative competence, and the education of disadvantaged children. *Anthropological Perspectives on Education.* Edited by M. Wax, S. Diamond and F. Gearing. New York: Basic Books, 1971.

_____ On communicative competence. *Sociolinguistics.* Edited by J. Pride and J. Holmes. London: Penguin Books, 1972.

_____ Models of interaction of language and social life. *Directions in Sociolinguistics: The Ethnology of Communication.* Edited by J.J. Gumperz and D. Hymes. New York: Holt, Rinehart and Winston, 1972.

_____ Sociolinguistics and the ethnography of speaking. *Language, Culture, and Society: A Book of Readings.* Edited by B.G. Blount. Cambridge, Mass.: Winthrop Publishers, 1974.

Imamoglu, E. Olcay. Children's awareness and usage of intention cues. *Child Development* 46 (1975): 39–45.

Inkeles, A. Social structure and the socialization of competence in socialization and schools. *Harvard Educational Review* (1968): 50–68.

Jackson, P.; Padover, C.; Dequine, M.; Price, K. *Beginning English Through Action (BETA).* Reading, Mass.: Addison-Wesley Publishing Co., 1982.

Jacobson, Rodolfo. Incorporating sociolinguistic norms into an EFL program. *TESOL Quarterly* X, 4 (December 1976): 411–422.

Jakobovits, Leon. The psychological bases of second-language learning. *Teaching the Bilingual.* Edited by F. Pialorsi. Tucson: University of Arizona Press, 1974.

Jarvis, Gilbert. The value of second-language learning. *Learning a Second Language Seventy-Ninth Yearbook of the National Society for the Study of Education Part II.* Edited by F. Grittner. Chicago: University of Chicago Press, 1980.

John, Vera. Cognitive development in the bilingual child. *Monograph Series on Languages and Linguistics.* Edited by J.E. Alatis. Washington, D.C.: Georgetown University Press, 1970.

Jolly, Yukiko S. The use of songs in teaching foreign languages. *Modern Language Journal* (January-February 1975): 11–14.

Jung, C.G. *The Development of Personality: The Collected Works of C.G. Jung (Volume 17).* Translated by R.F.C. Hull. Edited by Herbert Read, Michael Fordham, Gerhard Adler and William McGuire. Princeton, N.J.: Princeton University Press, 1974.

Kagan, Jerome; Moss, A. and Segal, I. Psychological significance of styles of conceptualization. *Monograph of the Society for Research in Child Development* 28 (1963): Serial No. 86.

Keenan, Elinor Ochs. The universality of conversational postulates. *Language in Society* 5 (April 1976): 67–80.

Keller-Cohen, Deborah and Dennis, James. The acquisition of conversational competence. *Functionalism.* Edited by R. Grossman et al. Chicago: Chicago Linguistic Society, 1975.

Kelley, G., ed. *Description and Measurement of Bilingualism: An International Seminar.* Toronto: Toronto Press, 1969.

Kirkton, Carole M. NCTE/ERIC report: classroom dramatics: developing oral language skills. *Elementary English* 46 (1969): 254–261.

Kleinjans, E. A question of ethics. *Exchange* 10, 4 (1975): 20–25.

Knapp, Mark L. The role of nonverbal communication in the classroom. *Theory Into Practice* (1975): 243–249.

Koch, Robert. The teacher and nonverbal communication. *Theory Into Practice* (1975): 231–241.

Kohn, James J. and Vajda, Peter G. Peer-mediated instruction and small-group interaction in the ESL classroom. *TESOL Quarterly* IX, 4 (December 1975): 379–390.

Kolers, P.A. Bilingualism and information processing. *Scientific American* 218 (1968): 78–87.

Krashen, Stephen D. Formal and informal linguistic environments in language acquisition and language learning. *TESOL Quarterly* X, 2 (June 1976): 157–168.

Kuchinskas, Gloria. Whose cognitive style makes the difference? *Educational Leadership* (January 1979): 269–271.

Kuhmerker, Lisa. When Sesame Street becomes Sesamstrasse: social education for preschoolers comes to television. *Social Education* (January 1976): 34–37.

Labov, William. *The Social Stratification of English in New York City (Urban Language Series)* Washington, D.C.: Center for Applied Linguistics, 1966.

_____ The study of language in its social context. *Studium Generale* XXIII (1970): 66–84.

_____ *Sociolinguistics Patterns.* Philadelphia: University of Pennsylvania Press, 1972.

_____ Rules for ritual insults. *Studies in Social Interaction.* Edited by D. Sudnow. New York: The Free Press, 1972.

Labov, William, Cohen, P. and Robbins, C. *A Preliminary Study of English Structure Used by Negro and Puerto Rican Speakers in New York City.* Final Report, Cooperative Research, Project No. 3091. Washington, D.C.: Office of Education, 1965.

Lambert, W.E. A social psychology of bilingualism. *Journal of Social Issues* 23 (1967): 91–109.

_____ Some cognitive consequences of following the curricula of the early school grades in a foreign language. *Monograph Series on Languages and Linguistics.* Edited by J.E. Alatis. Washington, D.C.: Georgetown University Press, 1970.

_____ *Language, Psychology, and Culture.* Stanford, Calif.: Stanford University Press, 1972.

Lambert, W.E. and Peal, E. The relations of bilingualism to intelligence. *Psychological Monographs* 5, 9 (1976).

Lambert, W.E. and Tucker, G.R. *Bilingual Education of Children: The St. Lambert Experiment.* Rowley, Mass.: Newbury House Publishers, 1972.

Lamendella, J.T. On the irrelevance of transformational grammar to second-language pedagogy. *Language Learning* 19 (1969): 270.

Laosa, L.M. Bilingualism in three United States Hispanic groups: contextual use of language by children and adults in their families. *Journal of Educational Psychology* 67 (1975): 617–627.

_____ Cognitive styles and learning strategies research: some of the areas in which psychology can contribute to personalized instruction in multicultural education. *Journal of Teacher Education* 28 (1977): 26–30.

_____ Socialization, education and continuity: the importance of the sociocultural context. *Young Children* 32 (1977): 21–27.

_____ Inequality in the classroom: observational research on teacher-student interactions. *Azlan-International Journal of Chicano Studies Research* 8 (1977): 51–67.

_____ Maternal teaching strategies in Chicano families of varied educational and socioeconomic levels. *Child Development* 49, 4 (December 1978): 1129–1135.

_____ Social competence in childhood: toward a developmental, socioculturally relativistic paradigm. *Primary Prevention of Psychopathology Vol. III: Social Competence in Children.* Edited by M.W. Kent and J.E. Rolf. Hanover, N.H.: University Press of New England, 1979.

Larsen-Freeman, Diane and Strom, Virginia. The construction of a second-language acquisition index of development. *Language Learning* XXVII, 1 (1977): 123–134.

Lawton, David. Chicano Spanish: some sociolinguistic considerations. *Bilingual Review* II, 1-2 (January-August 1975): 22–33.

Leahy, Robert L. and Huard, Carolyn. Role taking and self-image disparity in children. *Developmental Psychology* XII, 6 (1976): 504–508.

Lee, Seong-Soo and Dobson, Leona N. From referents to symbols: visual cues and pointing effects on children's acquisition of linear function rules. *Journal of Educational Psychology* LXIX, 5 (1977): 620–629.

Lenneberg, E.H. Language in the context of growth and maturation. *Biological Foundations of Language.* New York: John Wiley and Sons, 1967.

Leonard, L. Relational meaning and the facilitation of slow learning children's language. *American Journal of Mental Development* (September 1975): 180–185.

Levin, Jack and Kimmel, Allan J. Gossip columns: media small talk. *Journal of Communication* 27, 1 (Winter 1977): 169–175.

Levine, Josie. Some sociolinguistic parameters for analysis of language-learning materials. *IRAL* XIV, 2 (May 1976): 1–28.

Littlewood, William. Role performance and language teaching. *IRAL* 13, 3 (August 1975): 1–10.

Lopez, M. and Young, R.K. The linguistic independence of bilinguals. *Journal of Experimental Psychology* 102 (1974): 981–983.

Lopez, M.; Hicks, R.E.; and Young, R.K. Retroactive inhibition in a bilingual A-B paradigm. *Journal of Experimental Psychology* 103 (1974): 85–90.

Lott, Bernard. Sociolinguistics and the teaching of English. *English Language Teaching* (July 1975): 271–277.

Love, M. and Roderick, Jessie A. Teacher nonverbal communication: the development and field study of an awareness unit. *Theory Into Practice* (1971): 295–299.

Lutz, Frank W. and Ramsey, Margaret A. Nondirective cues as ritualistic indicators in educational organizations. *Education and Urban Society* (May 1973): 345–365.

Lynch, Charles Henry. An investigation of the relationship between conceptual ability and semantic generalizations. *Dissertation Abstracts* 21 (1961): 2799–2800.

Mackey, William F. *Bilingual Education in a Binational School.* Rowley, Mass.: Newbury House Publishers, 1972.

_____ How bilingualism has been described and measured. *Teaching the Bilingual.* Edited by F. Pialorsi. Tucson: University of Arizona Press, 1974.

MacNamara, John. The effects of instruction in a weaker language. *Journal of Social Issues* 2 (1967): 121–135.

_____ The linguistic independence of bilinguals. *Journal of Verbal Learning and Verbal Behavior* 6 (1967): 729–736.

_____ Bilingualism and thought. *Monograph Series on Languages and Linguistics.* Edited by J. Alatis. Washington, D.C.: Georgetown University Press, 1970.

_____ The cognitive strategies of language learning. *Focus on the Learner: Pragmatic Perspectives for the Language Teacher.* Edited by J.W. Oller, Jr. and J.C. Richards. Rowley, Mass.: Newbury House Publishers, 1973.

_____ What can we expect of a bilingual program? Paper read at the Second International Conference on Bilingual and Bicultural Education, New York, May, 1974.

MacNamara, John and Kushner, S.L. Linguistic independence of bilinguals: the input switch. *Journal of Verbal Learning and Verbal Behavior* 10, 5 (October 1971): 480–487.

Maize, Ray. A study in two methods of teaching composition. Ph.D. dissertation. Purdue University, 1952.

Maki, Ruth H. Recall as a function of the relationship between the cues and the words to be remembered. *American Journal of Psychology* XC, 2 (June 1977): 281–289.

Malherbe, E.G. *The Bilingual School.* London: Longmans, 1943.

Manzo, A.V. and Legenza, A. A method for assessing the language stimulation value of pictures. *Language Arts* (1975): 1085–1089.

Markman, Ellen M. Realizing that you don't understand: a preliminary investigation. *Child Development* 48 (1977): 986–992.

Martlew, M. et al. Language use, role and context in a five-year-old. *Journal of Child Language* 5, 1 (February 1978): 81–99.

McLaughlin, Barry. *Second-Language Acquisition in Childhood.* New Jersey: Lawrence Erlbaum Associates, 1978.

Menyuk, Paula. *Sentences Children Use.* Cambridge, Mass.: MIT Press, 1969.

Miller, G.A. The acquisition of word meaning. *Child Development* 49 (1978): 999–1004.

Miller, G.A., ed. *Communication, Language and Meaning: Psychological Perspectives*. New York: Basic Books, 1973.

Miller, Scott A. and Brownell, Celia A. Peers, persuasion, and Piaget: dyadic interaction between conservers and nonconservers. *Child Development* 46 (1975): 992–997.

Modiano, Nancy. Cultural and sociological factors relating to learning development. *ERIC*, ed. 010 924, 1966.

Moerk, Ernst L. Piaget's research as applied to the explanation of language development. *Merrill-Palmer Quarterly* XXI, 3 (1975): 153–169.

Moffett, James and Wagner, Betty Jane. *Student-Centered Language Arts and Reading K-13*. Boston: Houghton Mifflin Co., 1976.

Monane, L. Producing effective bilinguals: language classroom techniques to facilitate code switching within socio-semantic context of everyday life. *Roundtable on Language and Linguistics: Current Issues in Bilingual Education*. Edited by J.E. Alatis. Washington, D.C.: Georgetown University Press, 1980.

Montessori, M. *The Montessori Methods: Scientific Pedagogy as Applied to Child Education in "The Children's Houses."* Translated by A.E. George. New York: Frederick A. Stokes Co., 1912.

———— *The Montessori Method*. Cambridge, Mass.: Robert Bentley Inc., 1965.

Mueller, R. and Baker, J.F. Games teachers and students play. *Clearinghouse* 46, 8 (April 1972): 493–496.

Mueller, Theodore. The development of curriculum materials for individualized foreign language instruction. *Conference on Individualizing Foreign Language Instruction*. Edited by H.B. Altman and R.L. Politzer. Final unpublished report.

Myers, Barbara and Goldstein, D. Cognitive development in bilingual and monolingual lower-class children. *Psychology in the Schools* XVI, 1 (January 1979): 137–142.

Naumann, Nancy. We got a new kid and he don't speak English. *Language Learning* (October 1976): 45–50.

Nedler, Shari E. Explorations in teaching English as a second language. *Young Children* (December 1975): 480–488.

Nelson, Katherine. Structure and strategy in learning to talk. *Monographs of the Society for Research in Child Development* 38 (1973): Serial No. 149.

Nelson, Thomas O. Repetition and depth of processing. *Journal of Verbal Learning and Verbal Behavior* 16 (1977): 151–171.

Oller, J.W., Jr. Language communication and second-language learning. *The Psychology of Second-Language Learning*. Edited by P. Pimsleur and T. Quinn. Cambridge: Cambridge University Press, 1971.

———— Cloze tests of second-language proficiency and what they measure. *Language Learning* XXXIII, 1 (1972): 105–119.

Oller, J.W., Jr. and Perkins, Kyle. Further comments on language proficiency as a source of variance in certain affective measures. *Language Learning* 28 (1978): 417–422.

Olsen, James. The verbal ability of the culturally different. *The Reading Teacher* (April 1965): 552–556.

Olson, D. Language and thought: aspects of a cognitive theory of semantics. *Psychological Review* 77 (1970): 257–273.

Olson, Edward G. Teacher's role in life-centering the curriculum. *Journal of Teacher Education* XXVIII, 4 (July-August 1977): 17.

Olson, G.M. Developmental changes in memory and the acquisition of language. *Cognitive Development and Acquisition of Language*. Edited by T.E. Moore. New York: Academic Press, 1973.

Osburn, E. Bess. Children's language: what does it reveal? *Elementary School Journal*. (May 1978): 339–344.

Osler, Sonia F.; Draxl, Marilynn; and Madden, John. The utilization of verbal and perceptual cues by preschool children in concept identification problems. *Child Development* 48 (1977): 1071–1074.

Palermo, D.S. Word associations and children's verbal behavior. *Advances in Child Development and Behavior (Volume 1)*. Edited by L.P. Lipsitt and C.C. Spiker. New York: Academic Press, 1963.

Palmer, H.E. *The Scientific Study and Teaching of Language*. Edited by D. Harper. London: Oxford University Press, 1968.

Papalia, Anthony. Students' learning styles in ascribing meaning to written and oral stimuli. *Hispania* LVIII, 1 (March 1975): 106–108.

Parker, Larry R. and French, Russell L. A description of student behavior: verbal and nonverbal. *Theory Into Practice* (1975): 276–281.

Parrott, Ray J. Linguo-stylistic analysis and the language classroom. *Russian Language Journal* (Spring 1976): 51–59.

Paulston, Christina Bratt. Linguistic and communicative competence. *TESOL Quarterly* 8, 4 (1974): 347–362.

Paulston, Christina Bratt and Bruder, M. *Teaching English as a Second Language: Techniques and Procedures*. Cambridge, Mass.: Winthrop Publishers, 1976.

Peirce, C.S. *Collected Papers of Charles Sanders Peirce (Volume 2)*. Cambridge, Mass.: Harvard University Press, 1932.

Pelto, G. and Pelto, P. *The Nature of Anthropology*. Columbus, Ohio: Charles Merrill Publishing Co., 1966.

Peretti, Peter. Social role as a structural functional concept: a theoretical position paper regarding the socialization of the individual into his social role. *Child Study Journal* 7, 4 (1977): 189–201.

Peterson, M.J.; Peterson, Laryn A.; and Ward-Hull, Christine. Rehearsing and retaining mental matrices. *Journal of Verbal Learning and Verbal Behavior* 16 (1977): 371–381.

Pflaum, Susanna. *The Development of Language and Reading in the Young Child*. Columbus, Ohio: Charles Merrill Publishing Co., 1974.

Piaget, J. *Play, Dreams and Imitation in Childhood*. New York: W.W. Norton, 1951.

_____ *The Origins of Intelligence in Children*. New York: International Universities Press, 1952.

_____ *The Child's Conception of the World*. Paterson, N.J.: Littlefield Co., 1960.

_____ *The Child's Conception of Number.* New York: W.W. Norton, 1965.

_____ *The Child's Conception of Time.* London: Rutledge, Kegan and Paul, 1969.

Piaget, J. and Gouin, D. *Intelligence and Affectivity in Early Childhood: An Experimental Study of J. Piaget's Object Concept and Object Relations.* New York: International Universities Press, 1965.

Pinnell, Gay S. Language in primary classrooms. *Theory Into Practice* XIV, 5 (1975): 318–327.

Postovsky, V. The effects of delay in oral practice at the beginning of second-language teaching. Ph.D. dissertation. University of California, Berkeley, 1970.

_____ On paradoxes in foreign language teaching. *Modern Language Journal* (March 1975): 18–21.

_____ Why not start speaking later? *Viewpoints on English as a Second Language.* Edited by M. Burt, H. Dulay and M. Finocchiaro. New York: Regents Publishing Co., 1977.

Poyatos, Fernando. Language in the context of total body communication. *Revista de Occidente* 168 (1976): 49–62.

Ramer, Andrya L.H. The function of imitation in child language. *Journal of Speech and Hearing Research* 19 (1976): 700–717.

Ramirez, A. and Stromquist, Nelly. ESL methodology and student language learning in bilingual elementary school. *TESOL Quarterly* 2 (1979): 145–158.

Ramirez, Manuel and Castaneda, Alfredo. *Cultural Democracy, Biocognitive Development and Education.* New York: Academic Press, 1974.

Ratner, Nancy and Bruner, Jerome. Games, social exchange and acquisition of language. *Journal of Child Language* 5 (October 1978): 391–401.

Reckinger, Nancy. Choice as a way to quality learning. *Educational Leadership* (January 1979): 255–256.

Richards, Regina G. Singing: a fun route to a second language. *The Reading Teacher* (December 1975): 283–285.

Ritter, Kenneth. The development of knowledge of an external retrieval cue strategy. *Child Development* 49 (1978): 1227–1230.

Rivers, W.M. *Speaking in Many Tongues: Essays in Foreign Language Teaching.* Rowley, Mass.: Newbury House Publishers, 1972. Expanded 2nd edition, 1976.

_____ Psychology and linguistics as bases for language pedagogy. *Learning a Second Language. Seventy-Ninth Yearbook of the National Society for the Study of Education, Part II.* Edited by F. Grittner. Chicago: Chicago University Press, 1980.

Rivers, W.M. and Temperly, M. *A Practical Guide to the Teaching of English.* New York: Oxford University Press, 1978.

Rohwer, W.D., Jr.; Lynch, S.; Levin, J.R.; and Suzuki, N. Grade level school strata and learning efficiency. *Journal of Educational Psychology* 5 (1967): 294–302.

Rosansky, Ellen J. The critical period for the acquisition of language: some cognitive developmental considerations. *Working Papers in Bilingualism, No. 6,* 1975.

Rosenbaum, Peter. Learning two by two. *Teacher* (March 1976): 58–59.

Rosenfeld, H.M. Instrumental affiliative functions of facial and gestural expressions. *Journal of Personality and Social Psychology* 4 (1966): 65–72.

_____ Nonverbal reciprocation of approval: an experimental analysis. *Journal of Experimental Social Psychology* 3 (1977): 102–111.

Rosenthal, Robert and Jacobson, Lenore. *Pygmalion in the Classroom*. New York: Holt, Rinehart and Winston, 1968.

Rubin, J. *National Bilingualism in Paraguay*. The Hague: Mouton, 1968.

_____ What the "good language learner" can teach us. *TESOL Quarterly* IX, 1 (March 1975): 41–51.

Sachs, Jacqueline and Devin, Judity. Young children's use of age-appropriate speech styles in social interaction and role-playing. *Journal of Child Language* 3 (February 1976): 81–97.

Sacks, James M. Psychodrama: an underdeveloped group resource. *Educational Technology* (February 1973): 37–39.

Santoni, Georges V. An integrated approach, through linguistic and cross-cultural exercises, to advanced conversation. *Foreign Language Annuals* (May 1974): 425–434.

Sapir, E. *Language*. New York: Harcourt Brace Javanovich, 1947.

Savignon, Sandra J. *Testing Communicative Competence*. Montreal: Marcel Didier, 1972.

Scarcella, Robin C. Sociodrama for social interaction. *TESOL Quarterly* XII, 1 (March 1978): 41–46.

Schachter, Frances Fuchs; Marquis, Ruth E.; Ganger, Sonia A.; and McCaffery, Regina M. Socialized speech: a proposed resolution of the controversy. *The Journal of Genetic Psychology* 130 (1977): 305–321.

Schneider, John E. Mind to mind communication: nonverbal influence? *Theory Into Practice* (1975): 259–263.

Schumann, J.H. Affective factors and the problem of age in second-language acquisition. *Language Learning* 25 (1975): 209–235.

Schwartz, Judy I. Teacher talk and pupil talk. *Language Arts* (September 10, 1975): 886–888.

Scotton, Carol Myers and Ury, William. Bilingual strategies: the social functions of code switching. *Linguistics* (June 1977): 5–20.

Seliger, H.W. Inductive and deductive method in language teaching: a re-examination. *International Review of Applied Linguistics* 13, 1 (1975).

_____ Does practice make perfect?: a study of interaction patterns in second-language competence. *Language Learning* 27, 2 (1977): 263–278.

Seliger, H.W. and Gingras, Rosario. Who speaks how much and to whom?: a study of interaction patterns in second-language classrooms. Paper read at Colloquium on Verbal and Nonverbal Behavior in Second-Language Learning, National TESOL Convention, New York, 1976.

Shaftel, Fannie. Role playing: an approach to meaningful social learning. *Social Education* 3, 4, 5 (May 1970): 556–559.

Shatz, M. and Gelman, R. The development of communication skills: modifications in the speech of young children as a function of listener. *Monographs of the Society for Research in Child Development* 38 (1973): Serial No. 152.

Sheldon, William D. and Lashinger, Donald R. A summary of research studies relating to language arts in elementary education: 1969. *Elementary English* (1971): 243–274.

Shepherd, Richard C. Oral language performance and reading instruction. *Elementary English* 51, 4 (1974): 544–556.

Shertzer, B. *Fundamentals of Counseling.* Boston: Houghton Mifflin Co., 1968.

Shiffrin, R.M. and Atkinson, R.C. Storage and retrieval processes in long term memory. *Psychological Review* 76, 2 (1969): 179–193.

Skinner, B.F. *Verbal Behavior.* New York: Appleton-Century-Crofts, 1957.

Siegel, S. *Diseno experimental, no-paramentrico.* Mexico, 1970.

Silva, Carmen. Recent theories of language acquisition in relation to a semantic approach in foreign language teaching. *English Language Teaching* (July 1975): 337–346.

Smitherman, Geneva. Soul and style. *English Journal* (February 1976): 14–16.

Sommer, Tamara. Culture in foreign language teaching. *Canadian Modern Language Review* XXX, 4 (May 1974): 342–346.

Sorenson, A.P. Multilingualism in the northwest Amazon. *American Anthropologist* 69 (1967): 670–684.

Stanford, Gene. Why role playing fails. *English Journal* 69, 9 (December 1974): 50–54.

Steinberg, Zina D. and Cazden, Courtney B. Children as teachers—of peers and ourselves. *Theory Into Practice* 18, 4 (October 1979): 258–266.

Stern, H.H. What can we learn from the good language learner? *Canadian Modern Language Review* (March 1975): 304–318.

Stewig, John Warren. Nonverbal communication: "I see what you say." *Language Arts* LVI, 2 (February 1979): 150–155.

Stieglitz, Francine B. *Teaching a Second Language: Sentence Length and Syntax.* NCTE Research Report No. 14, 1973.

Strom, Robert and Ray, William. Communication in the affective domain. *Theory Into Practice* (1975): 268–275.

Swain, James. E. Is listening really more effective for learning in the early grades? *Elementary English* 50 (November-December 1973): 1110–1113.

Swenson, Ingrid. Word recognition cues used in matching verbal stimuli within and between auditory and visual modalities. *Journal of Educational Psychology* LXVII, 3 (1975): 409–415.

Szentivaniyi, Agnes. Communicative situations in the training of teachers of ESL. *English Language Training* XXX (April 1976): 179–184.

Taylor, Barry P. Adult language learning strategies and their pedagogical implications. *TESOL Quarterly* IX, 4 (December 1975): 391–399.

Taylor, Barry P. and Wolfson, Nessa. Breaking down the free conversation myth. *TESOL Quarterly* XII, 1 (March 1978): 31–39.

Taylor, H.J.S. Teach your pupils to gossip. *English Language Teaching* (April 1977): 222–226.

Terrell, Tracy D. A natural approach to second-language acquisition and learning. *Modern Language Journal* 61 (November 1977): 325–337.

Tovey, D.R. The psycholinguistic guessing game. *Language Arts* 53, 3 (March 1976): 319–322.

Troike, Muriel. Language drill and young children. *Teaching the Bilingual.* Edited by F. Pialorsi. Tucson: University of Arizona Press, 1974.

Tucker, G.R. Affective, cognitive and social factors in second-language acquisition. *Canadian Modern Language Review* 32, 3 (February 1976): 218–226.

Tucker, Richard. An alternate days approach to bilingual education. *Monograph Series on Languages and Linguistics.* Edited by J.E. Alatis. Washington, D.C.: Georgetown University Press, 1970.

Tulving, E. and Thomson, D.M. Encoding specificity and retrieval processes in episodic memory. *Psychological Review* 80 (1973): 352–373.

Tulving, E. and Donaldson, W., eds. *Organization of Memory.* New York: Academic Press, 1972.

Turner, Richard L. The value of variety in teaching styles. *Educational Leadership* (January 1979): 257–258.

Twaddell, F. Vocabulary expansion in the TESOL classroom. *TESOL Quarterly* 7, 1 (March 1973): 61–78.

Ulatowska, Hanna K. and Scott, Winfield H. Linguistic indicators of perceptual style. *Linguistics* 105 (June 1, 1973): 83–90.

Valette, R.M. Some reflections on second language in young children. *Language Learning* 14 (1964): 91–98.

Wagner, Betty Jane. The use of role. *Language Arts* LV, 3 (March 1978): 323–327.

―――― Using drama to create an environment for language development. *Language Arts* LVI, 3 (March 1979): 268–274.

Waller, S. *The Sociology of Teaching.* New York: John Wiley and Sons, 1967.

Ward, C.O.; Zanna, M.P.; and Cooper, J. The nonverbal mediation of self-fulfilling prophecies in interracial interaction. *Journal of Experimental Social Psychology* 19, 2 (1974): 109–120.

Watson, K.A. Transferable communicative routines: strategies and group identity in two special events. *Language in Society* 4, 1 (April 1975): 53–72.

Weaver, Susan W. and Rutherford, William L. A hierarchy of listening skills. *Elementary English* 50 (November-December 1976): 1146–1149.

Weiner, Morton; Devoe, Shannon; Rubinow, Stuart; and Geller, Jesse. Nonverbal behavior and nonverbal communication. *Psychological Review* LXXIX, 3 (May 1972): 185–213.

Weir, R.H. *Language in the Crib.* The Hague: Mouton, 1962.

Welkowitz, J.; Cariffe, D.; and Feldstein, S. Conversational congruence as a criterion of socialization in children. *Child Development* 47 (1976): 269–272.

Wells, David J. Role playing in the foreign language class. *French Review* (March 1975): 760–763.

Wells, Gordon. Learning to code experience through language. *Journal of Child Language* 1 (June 1976): 243–269.

Werner, H. *Comparative Psychology of Mental Development.* Revised edition. Chicago: Follett Publishing Co., 1948.

Whitehurst, G.J. The development of communication: changes with age and modeling. *Child Development* 47 (1976): 473–482.

_____ Comprehension, selective initiation, and the CIP hypothesis. *Journal of Experimental Child Psychology* 23 (1977): 23–38.

_____ The contributions of social learning to language acquisition. *Contemporary Educational Psychology* 3 (1978): 2–10.

_____ *The Functions of Language and Cognition.* New York: Academic Press, 1979.

Whitehurst, G.J. and Merkur, Anita E. The development of communication: modeling and contrast failure. *Child Development* 48 (1977): 993–1001.

Whitehurst, G.J. and Vasta, R. Is language acquired through imitation? *Journal of Psycholinguistic Research* 4 (1975): 37–59.

Williams, Frederick. The identification of linguistic attitudes. *Linguistics* (September 1974): 21–32.

Witbeck, Michael C. Peer correction procedures for intermediate and advanced ESL composition lessons. *TESOL Quarterly* X, 3 (September 1976): 321–326.

Witkin, Herman. Cognitive style approach to cross cultural research. *International Journal of Psychology* 2 (1967): 233–250.

Wolfson, Nessa. Speech events and natural speech: some implications for sociolinguistic methodology. *Language in Society* (August 1976): 189–209.

Wyche, La Monte G. A critique of studies on the effect of social experience on language development. *The Journal of Negro Education* XLVIII, 2 (1979): 182–186.

Wynne, Edward A. Schools and socialization. *Educational Leadership* (April 1979): 464–468.

Yussen, Steven R.; Kunen, Seth; and Buss, Ray. The distinction between perceiving and memorizing in the presence of category cues. *Child Development* 46 (1975): 763–768.

Zampogna, Joseph; Gentile, Ronald J.; Papalia, Anthony; and Silber, Gordon R. Relationships between learning styles and learning environments in selected modern language classes. *Modern Language Journal* (December 1976): 443–447.

Zentella, A.C. Code-switching and interactions among Puerto Rican children. *Working Papers in Sociolinguistics, No. 50.* Southwest Educational Development Lab, Austin, Texas. ERIC Document ED 165 493, 1978.